SUMMER MATH WORKBOOK

Bridge Building Activities

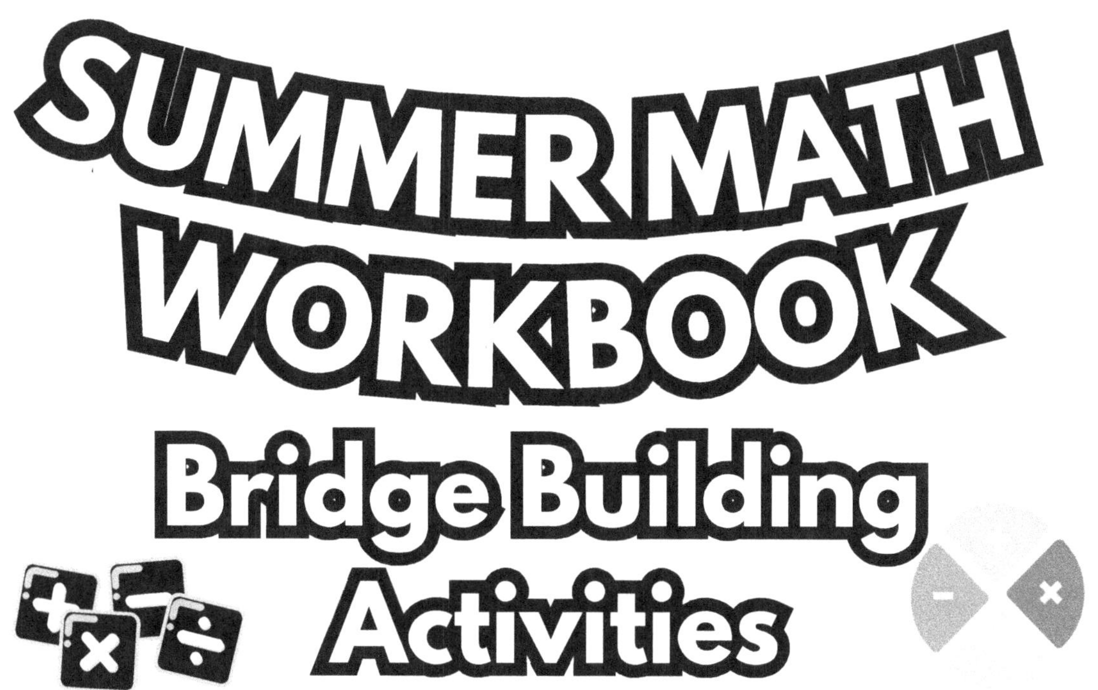

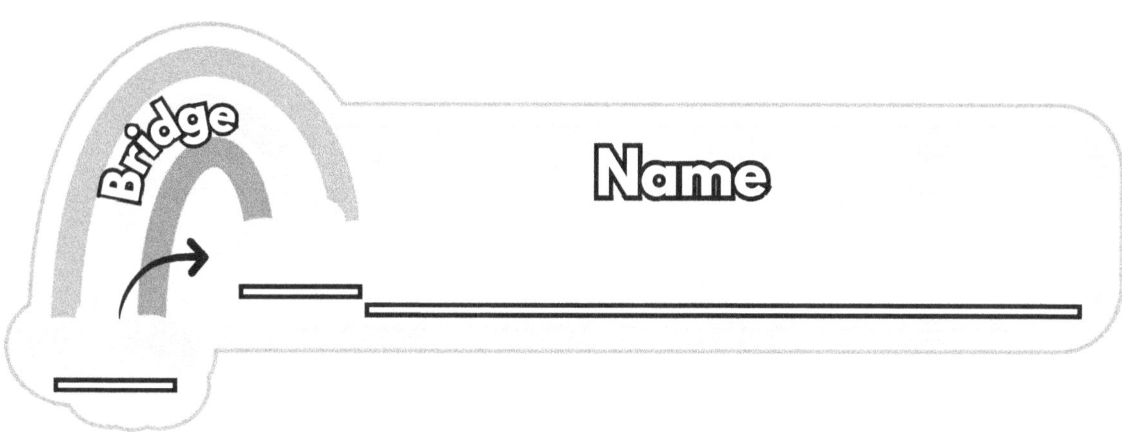

<u>Introduction</u>

As parents and educators, we understand the pivotal role that mathematics plays in shaping a child's academic journey and future success. Yet, the path to mathematical proficiency can often seem daunting, filled with challenges and complexities. That's where the transformative power of Summer Bridge Building Activities books comes into play, illuminating the way forward with clarity, precision, and purpose.

Summer vacation is a time for rest and relaxation, but it also presents the risk of the "summer slide," where students lose some of the academic gains they made during the school year. Summer Bridge Building Activities books are specifically designed to tackle this challenge, ensuring that your child stays academically engaged and prepared for the upcoming school year. These books provide a seamless bridge from one grade to the next, reinforcing essential skills and introducing new concepts that will give your child a head start.

Imagine your child eagerly diving into the pages of a Summer Bridge Building Activities book, greeted by clear, engaging content that demystifies complex mathematical concepts. With each turn of the pages, they embark on a journey of discovery, encountering thoughtfully curated practice questions that reinforce learning and sharpen problem-solving skills. As they unveil the answers to those questions, a sense of accomplishment blossoms within them — a tangible reward for their hard work and dedication.

Summer Bridge Building Activities books transcend traditional educational tools; they are meticulously crafted to build a deep and enduring understanding of mathematics. These books follow a sequential and logical progression, starting from fundamental principles and advancing to sophisticated problem-solving strategies. Each chapter is designed to build on the previous one, ensuring a solid and comprehensive foundation for future learning.

Parents, we yearn for nothing more than to see our children thrive academically and personally. We want to witness the spark of inspiration ignited within them as they overcome academic challenges with confidence and poise. Summer Bridge Building Activities books serve as indispensable partners in this noble endeavor, offering not just practice questions but the keys to unlocking a world of academic and personal opportunities.

Visualize the pride on your child's face as they master a challenging math concept, the joy they experience when their efforts yield results, and the confidence they gain with each success. These pages are designed to make learning math a positive, enriching, and deeply rewarding experience that will benefit them throughout their academic journey and beyond.

For educators, Summer Bridge Building Activities books are invaluable allies in the quest to cultivate mathematical proficiency in the classroom. Accompanied by comprehensive guides and readily available answers, instructors can focus on mentoring and nurturing their students, secure in the knowledge that these books provide a robust framework for effective learning.

Within the pages of Summer Bridge Building Activities books lies not just the promise of academic excellence, but the seeds of a brighter future. By integrating these resources into your child's summer routine, you are bestowing upon them the gifts of confidence, curiosity, and a lifelong love of learning.

Invest in your child's future today with Summer Bridge Building Activities books — because every great journey begins with a single step, and this step can change everything. Keep the momentum of learning alive over the summer, and watch your child soar to new academic heights.

Contents

Grade
1 → 2
SUMMER MATH WORKBOOK
Bridge Building Activities
Number Sense
Addition and Subtraction
Place Value

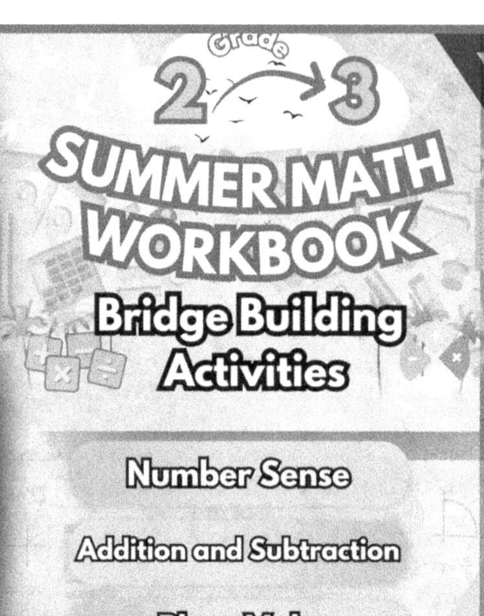

Grade
2 → 3
SUMMER MATH WORKBOOK
Bridge Building Activities
Number Sense
Addition and Subtraction
Place Value

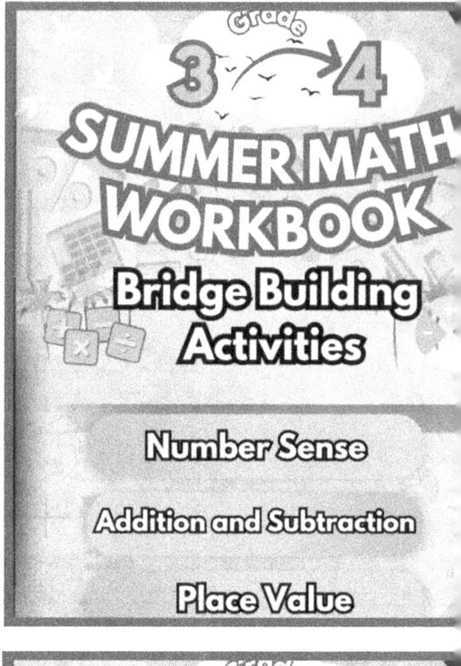

Grade
3 → 4
SUMMER MATH WORKBOOK
Bridge Building Activities
Number Sense
Addition and Subtraction
Place Value

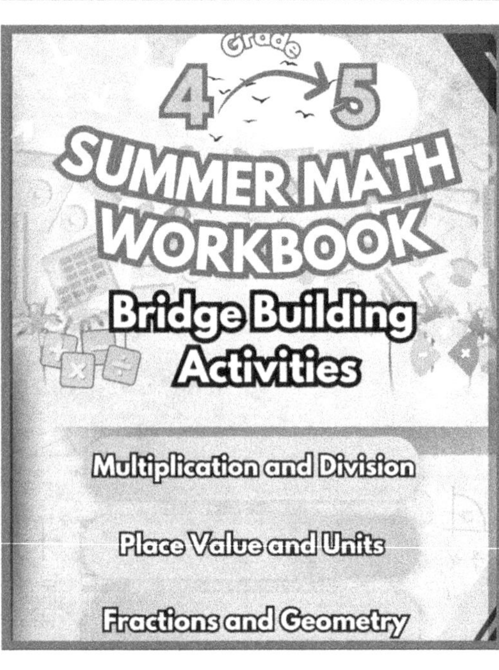

Grade
4 → 5
SUMMER MATH WORKBOOK
Bridge Building Activities
Multiplication and Division
Place Value and Units
Fractions and Geometry

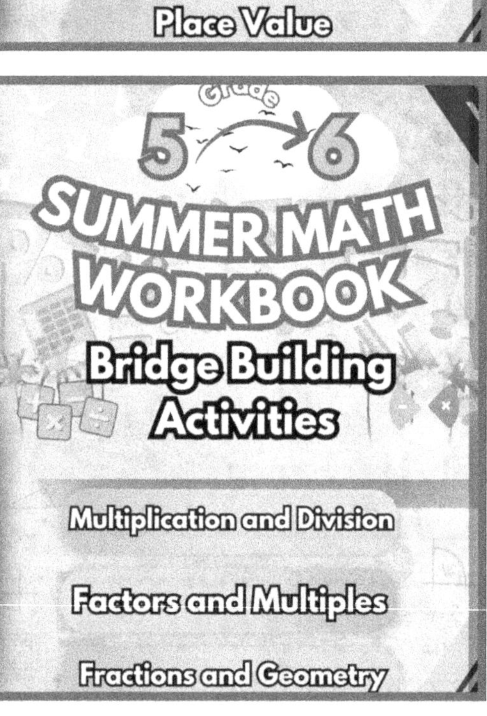

Grade
5 → 6
SUMMER MATH WORKBOOK
Bridge Building Activities
Multiplication and Division
Factors and Multiples
Fractions and Geometry

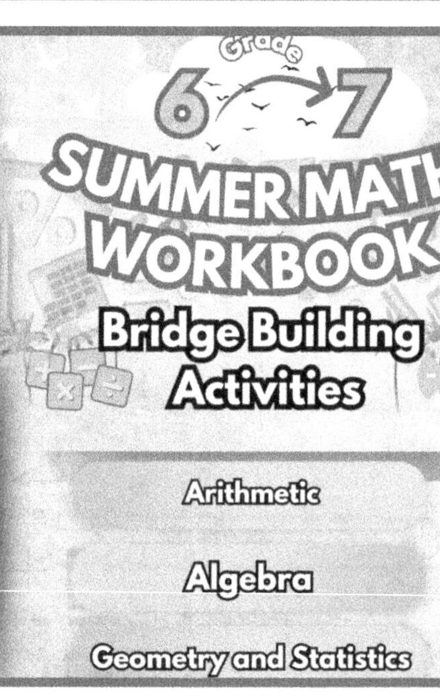

Grade
6 → 7
SUMMER MATH WORKBOOK
Bridge Building Activities
Arithmetic
Algebra
Geometry and Statistics

Grade
7 → 8
SUMMER MATH WORKBOOK
Bridge Building Activities
Ratio and Percentage
Algebra and Cartesian Plane
Geometry and Statistics

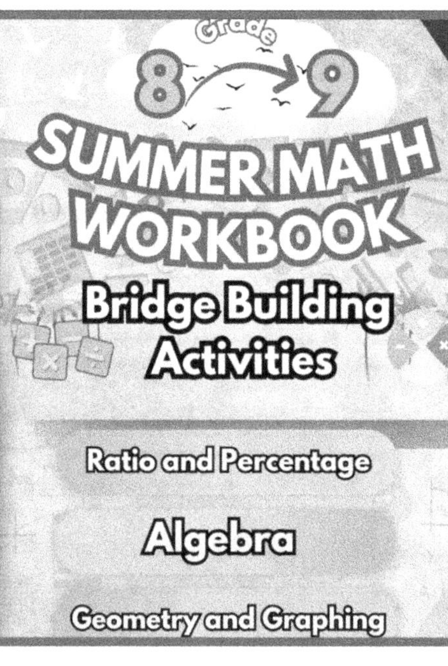

Grade
8 → 9
SUMMER MATH WORKBOOK
Bridge Building Activities
Ratio and Percentage
Algebra
Geometry and Graphing

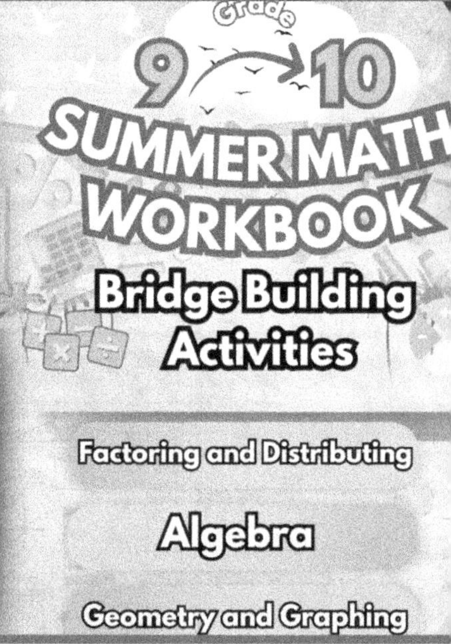

Grade
9 → 10
SUMMER MATH WORKBOOK
Bridge Building Activities
Factoring and Distributing
Algebra
Geometry and Graphing

Addition and Subtraction

Addition with Regrouping

When we add numbers, sometimes the sum in a place value column is greater than 9. In this case, we need to regroup. Regrouping means moving a ten to the tens place or a hundred to the hundreds place.

Example: Let's add 278 and 156.

$$278$$
$$+\underline{156}$$

First, we add the ones place: $8 + 6 = 14$. We write down the 4 in the ones place and carry-over the 1 to the tens place.

$$1$$
$$278$$
$$+\underline{156}$$
$$4$$

Next, we add the tens place, including the carry-over: $1 + 7 + 5 = 13$. We write down the 3 in the tens place and carry-over the 1 to the hundreds place.

$$11$$
$$278$$
$$+\underline{156}$$
$$34$$

Finally, we add the hundreds place, including the carry-over: $1 + 2 + 1 = 4$.

$$\begin{array}{r} 1\ 1 \\ 2\ 7\ 8 \\ +\ 1\ 5\ 6 \\ \hline 4\ 3\ 4 \end{array}$$

Subtraction with Regrouping

Sometimes when we subtract, the top digit in a place value column is smaller than the bottom digit. In this case, we need to regroup. Regrouping means borrowing from the next column.

Example: Let's subtract 195 from 322.

$$\begin{array}{r} 3\ 2\ 2 \\ -\ 1\ 9\ 5 \\ \hline \end{array}$$

First, we subtract the ones place: 2 - 5. Since 2 is smaller than 5, we need to regroup. We borrow 1 from the tens place, making it 1 ten instead of 2, and add it to the ones place, making it 12.

$$\begin{array}{r} 2\ 12 \\ 3\ 2\ 2 \\ -\ 1\ 9\ 5 \\ \hline 7 \end{array}$$

Next, we subtract the tens place: 1 - 9. Since 1 is smaller than 9, we need to regroup again. We borrow 1 from the hundreds place, making it 2 hundreds instead of 3, and add it to the tens place, making it 11.

$$\begin{array}{r} 11 \\ 2\ 12 \\ 3\ 2\ 2 \\ -\ 1\ 9\ 5 \\ \hline 2\ 7 \end{array}$$

Finally, we subtract the hundreds place: 2 - 1 = 1

$$
\begin{array}{r}
11 \\
2\ 12 \\
3\ 2\ 2 \\
-1\ 9\ 5 \\
\hline
1\ 2\ 7
\end{array}
$$

<h1 align="center">Multiplication</h1>

Multiplication

Multiplication simplifies the process of adding numbers repeatedly. Instead of repeatedly adding the same number, we use multiplication for a quicker result.

For example, rather than adding 3 + 3 + 3 + 3, we can multiply 3 by 4 to get the same result: $3 \times 4 = 12$. Here, 3 is the multiplicand, 4 is the multiplier, and 12 is the product.

Think of multiplication as repeated addition. For instance, 3×4 means adding 3 four times: 3 + 3 + 3 + 3 = 12.

We can also visualize multiplication as groups of objects. Imagine 3 groups, each containing 4 apples. To find the total number of apples, multiply the number of groups (3) by the number of apples in each group (4): 3 groups of 4 apples = 12 apples. Expressed as multiplication: $3 \times 4 = 12$.

Division

Division is the inverse operation of multiplication. It involves sharing or distributing items equally among a certain number of groups or people.

When we divide one number by another, we split it into equal parts, determining how many groups of a specific size can be made from that number.

For instance, let's divide 24 by 6. This means we're asking, "How many groups of size 6 can we make from 24?"

The key terms in division are:

- **Dividend**: The number being divided (24 in this case).
- **Divisor**: The number we are dividing by (6 in this case).

- **Quotient**: The result of the division, indicating how many groups of the divisor fit into the dividend (4 in this case).

So, when we divide 24 by 6, we find that 4 groups of 6 can be made from 24.

Place Value and Expanded Notation

Place value tells us the value of a digit in a number based on where it's placed.

Imagine we have the number 45,643. It has five digits: 4, 5, 6, 4, and 3.

Digit	Place Value Position	Value Calculation	Value
4	Ten thousands place	$4 \times 10{,}000$	40,000
5	Thousands place	$5 \times 1{,}000$	5,000
6	Hundreds place	6×100	600
4	Tens place	4×10	40
3	Ones place	3×1	3

Each digit occupies a unique position. By summing these values, we determine the overall value of the number:

$$40{,}000 + 5{,}000 + 600 + 40 + 3 = 45{,}643$$

<u>**Geometry**</u>

Area and Perimeter

The area of a shape measures the amount of space it occupies, while the perimeter is the total distance around its boundary.

Area of a Square

For a square, where all four sides are equal, we only need to know the length of one side to find its area. We calculate the area by squaring the length of one side. If the length of a side is 's', then the area (A) is:

$$A = s^2$$

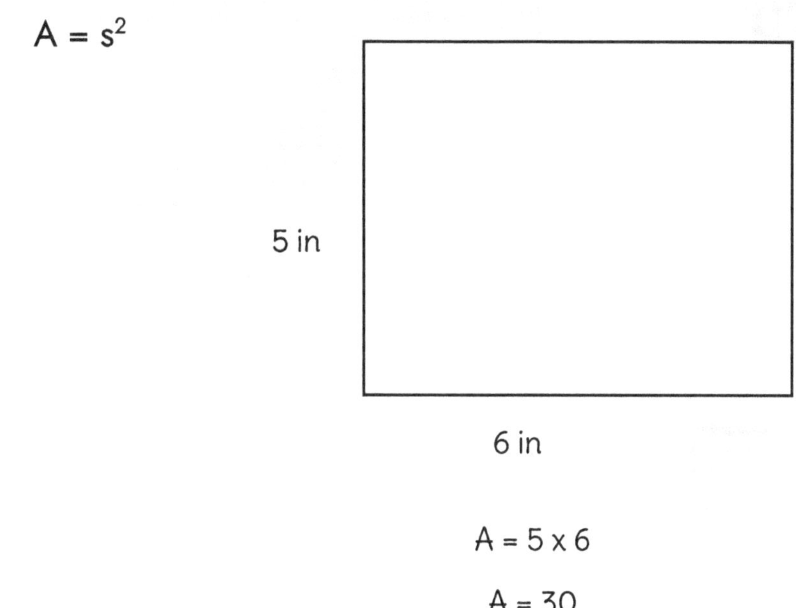

$$A = 5 \times 6$$

$$A = 30$$

Perimeter of Rectangle

To find the perimeter (P) of a square, multiply the length of one side by 4. For a side length 's', the perimeter is:

$$P=4s$$

$$P = 4 \times s$$

$$P = 5 \times 6$$

$$P = 30$$

Area of a Rectangle

For a rectangle, the area is found by multiplying its length (l) by its width (w). The formula is:

$$A = l \times w$$

Perimeter of a Rectangle

The perimeter of a rectangle is obtained by summing the lengths of all four sides. The formula is:

$$P = 2l + 2w$$

Area of Triangle:

The area of a triangle represents the amount of space enclosed within its three sides. The formula for calculating the area of a triangle depends on the type of triangle. For a general triangle, we use the formula:

$$A = \frac{1}{2} \times base \times height$$

Where:

- A represents the area of the triangle.

- The base is the length of any one side of the triangle.

- The height is the perpendicular distance from the base to the opposite vertex.

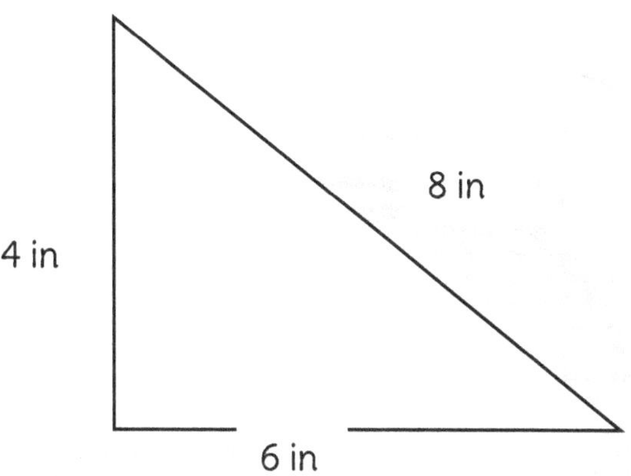

$$A = \frac{1}{2} \times \text{base} \times \text{height}$$

$$A = \frac{1}{2} \times 4 \times 6$$

$$A = \frac{1}{2} \times 24$$

$$A = 12$$

Perimeter of Triangle:

The perimeter of a triangle is the total length of its three sides. To calculate the perimeter, add the lengths of all three sides together:

$$P = \text{side1} + \text{side2} + \text{side3}$$

For example, if the lengths of the sides are 4, 6, and 8, then:

$$P = 4 + 6 + 8 = 18$$

Counting Patterns: Count by 5s

Complete the counting tables.

1. Count by 5 from 359 to 379

359	364	369	374	379

2. Count by 5 from 844 to 864

				864

3. Count by 5 from 743 to 763

743				

4. Count by 5 from 333 to 353

		343		

5. Count by 5 from 91 to 111

			106	

6. Count by 5 from 634 to 654

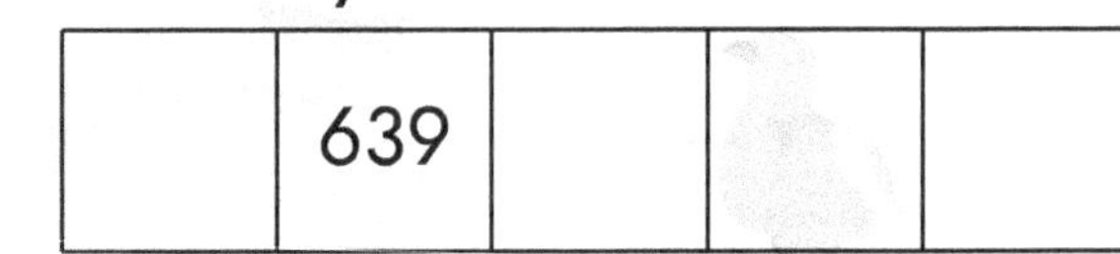

	639			

7. Count by 5 from 317 to 337

				337

8. Count by 5 from 616 to 636

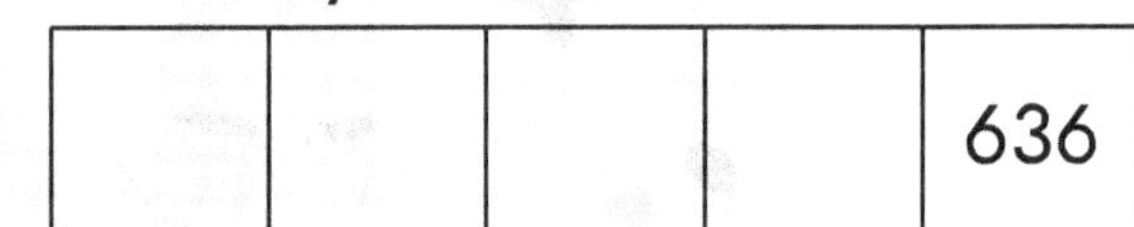

				636

9. Count by 5 from 136 to 156

				156

10. Count by 5 from 483 to 503

		493		

11. Count by 5 from 459 to 479

459				

12. Count by 5 from 612 to 632

612				

13. Count by 5 from 101 to 121

		111		

14. Count by 5 from 202 to 222

202				

15. Count by 5 from 951 to 971

				971

16. Count by 5 from 361 to 381

				381

17. Count by 5 from 395 to 415

		405		

18. Count by 5 from 345 to 365

			360	

19. Count by 5 from 367 to 387

367				

20. Count by 5 from 837 to 857

			852	

21. Count by 5 from 801 to 821

	806			

22. Count by 5 from 174 to 194

		184		

23. Count by 5 from 815 to 835

			830	

24. Count by 5 from 33 to 53

		43		

25. Count by 5 from 141 to 161

	146			

26. Count by 5 from 9 to 29

	14			

27. Count by 5 from 144 to 164

				164

28. Count by 5 from 214 to 234

	219			

29. Count by 5 from 116 to 136

				136

30. Count by 5 from 454 to 474

454				

31. Count by 5 from 752 to 772

				772

32. Count by 5 from 461 to 481

461				

33. Count by 5 from 404 to 424

				424

34. Count by 5 from 690 to 710

			705	

35. Count by 5 from 878 to 898

				898

36. Count by 5 from 698 to 718

698				

37. Count by 5 from 537 to 557

		547		

38. Count by 5 from 279 to 299

			294	

Counting Patterns: Count by 10s

Complete the counting tables.

1. Count by 10 from 765 to 805

765	775	785	795	805

2. Count by 10 from 716 to 756

			746	

3. Count by 10 from 639 to 679

				679

4. Count by 10 from 527 to 567

	537			

5. Count by 10 from 213 to 253

	223			

6. Count by 10 from 215 to 255

		235		

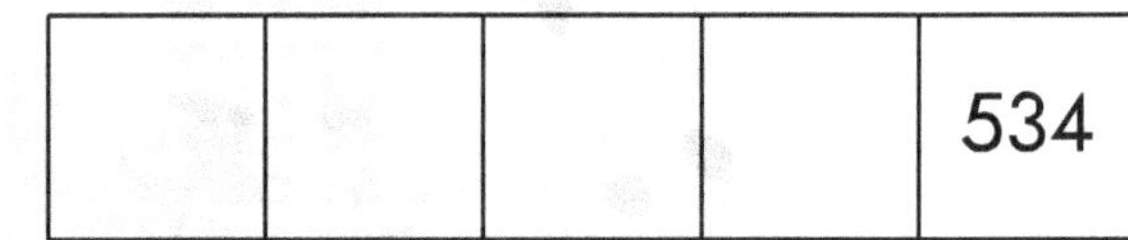

7. Count by 10 from 750 to 790

			780	

8. Count by 10 from 494 to 534

				534

9. Count by 10 from 835 to 875

			865	

10. Count by 10 from 911 to 951

				951

11. Count by 10 from 372 to 412

				412

12. Count by 10 from 175 to 215

			205	

13. Count by 10 from 609 to 649

		629		

14. Count by 10 from 468 to 508

			488	

15. Count by 10 from 464 to 504

		484		

16. Count by 10 from 514 to 554

		524		

17. Count by 10 from 278 to 318

	288			

18. Count by 10 from 636 to 676

			656	

19. Count by 10 from 578 to 618

578				

20. Count by 10 from 424 to 464

	434			

21. Count by 10 from 130 to 170

130				

22. Count by 10 from 647 to 687

				687

23. Count by 10 from 61 to 101

				101

24. Count by 10 from 586 to 626

586				

25. Count by 10 from 503 to 543

				543

26. Count by 10 from 984 to 1024

			1,014	

27. Count by 10 from 880 to 920

			910	

28. Count by 10 from 246 to 286

			276	

29. Count by 10 from 848 to 888

				888

30. Count by 10 from 173 to 213

			203	

31. Count by 10 from 370 to 410

370				

32. Count by 10 from 316 to 356

			346	

33. Count by 10 from 777 to 817

		797		

34. Count by 10 from 551 to 591

551				

35. Count by 10 from 289 to 329

289				

36. Count by 10 from 476 to 516

		496		

37. Count by 10 from 341 to 381

		361		

38. Count by 10 from 16 to 56

	26			

Comparing the Numbers

Add: > or < or = to make the following statements true.

1. 7,166 < 7,260

2. 4,335 _____ 8,177

3. 4,785 _____ 1,684

4. 5,778 _____ 9,008

5. 8,265 _____ 8,166

6. 6,127 _____ 3,573

7. 6,048 _____ 6,565

8. 1,797 _____ 6,418

9. 4,655 _____ 8,985

10. 5,350 _____ 5,480

11. 7,070 _____ 4,900

12. 4,049 _____ 5,524

13. 9,115 _____ 8,438

14. 2,669 _____ 8,491

15. 9,334 _____ 9,786

16. 7,379 _____ 2,234

17. 6,321 _______ 9,097

18. 9,778 _______ 4,590

19. 2,393 _______ 3,350

20. 2,270 _______ 8,470

21. 1,015 _______ 1,676

22. 7,698 _______ 2,900

23. 2,464 _______ 2,085

24. 2,196 _______ 1,002

25. 9,808 _______ 2,408

26. 8,844 _______ 5,414

27. 5,019 _______ 9,367

28. 5,895 _______ 3,266

29. 4,210 _______ 8,811

30. 9,062 _______ 6,346

31. 9,014 _______ 7,286

32. 9,673 _______ 8,478

33. 1,787 _______ 4,893

34. 7,251 _______ 6,950

35. 6,787 _______ 7,207

36. 5,025 _______ 2,304

37. 7,714 _______ 6,879

38. 5,464 _______ 6,393

39. 7,202 _______ 2,149

40. 4,059 _______ 8,030

41. 7,242 _______ 2,666

42. 8,683 _______ 7,926

43. 1,942 _______ 2,964

44. 7,215 _______ 6,953

45. 4,202 _______ 7,512

46. 1,379 _______ 3,581

47. 4,288 _______ 5,923

48. 9,455 _______ 3,729

49. 2,002 _______ 9,220

50. 2,113 _______ 7,571

Circle the Numbers

Circle the smallest and biggest number in each group.

1. 6,291   8,564   5,421   9,711
2. 4,210   2,604   8,051   8,549

3. 8,733   2,289   6,289   3,449
4. 7,112   8,262   2,323   4,765

5. 9,936   6,400   5,557   8,974
6. 2,783   5,280   3,668   8,174

7. 6,607   5,386   4,212   6,599
8. 9,257   5,200   1,244   8,362

9. 9,457   4,461   3,218   6,051
10. 1,337   6,260   2,105   6,005

11. 8,084   7,749   9,011   5,306
12. 4,372   8,050   7,398   2,046

13. 4,281   1,112   9,420   2,958
14. 5,326   1,616   2,581   2,010

15. 5,895   7,246   4,104   8,823
16. 8,391   2,451   9,291   4,532

17. 2,045 7,926 3,992 3,651

18. 6,043 6,272 4,427 4,675

19. 5,294 9,552 1,889 5,034

20. 6,269 8,362 4,802 8,556

21. 7,988 3,166 3,318 9,145

22. 5,780 8,286 4,036 8,840

23. 2,879 2,207 1,155 4,090

24. 3,156 3,282 7,613 6,633

25. 8,457 5,478 4,260 6,445

26. 5,058 4,747 6,002 8,008

27. 6,684 5,744 7,663 5,773

28. 9,726 7,547 5,741 7,532

29. 3,444 5,547 1,835 6,225

30. 9,132 1,146 8,752 3,758

31. 4,890 5,151 1,771 4,835

32. 6,116 1,336 2,519 3,012

33. 2,939 5,256 6,577 1,791

34. 5,101 8,356 4,498 4,240

35. 7,163 5,309 3,460 1,035   **36.** 1,623 8,262 9,114 5,332

37. 6,466 3,622 1,646 7,608   **38.** 2,446 2,388 7,500 8,310

39. 6,725 1,501 2,555 9,907   **40.** 3,975 2,166 2,892 6,348

41. 4,225 5,650 3,834 5,470   **42.** 1,969 4,950 3,431 5,088

43. 2,049 7,594 9,061 4,823   **44.** 7,686 8,717 3,135 6,627

45. 6,037 6,439 8,369 3,493   **46.** 9,690 4,910 1,566 1,551

47. 7,755 8,267 5,065 4,599   **48.** 6,801 4,591 1,265 5,996

49. 3,417 7,112 6,809 5,972   **50.** 5,428 4,643 4,362 2,515

Circle the Numbers

Circle the odd numbers in each group.

1. 1,191   6,557   6,559   4,851
2. 3,327   3,677   1,623   8,007

3. 8,366   (5,927)   4,870   7,536
4. 3,797   9,398   6,657   9,314

5. 5,084   3,282   7,715   3,702
6. 9,884   8,831   8,287   7,457

7. 7,329   4,064   2,406   1,574
8. 2,907   7,163   2,198   2,393

9. 3,076   6,853   3,302   4,132
10. 8,350   6,714   8,224   5,078

11. 7,643   7,057   6,233   1,873
12. 9,721   3,728   3,199   4,018

13. 1,454   7,494   1,888   3,145
14. 6,928   1,660   2,631   2,360

15. 8,270   9,101   7,522   9,262
16. 2,271   1,049   6,099   2,202

17. 4,729   3,476   5,460   6,944

18. 7,096   3,525   1,963   8,370

19. 5,058   3,636   6,059   3,827

20. 3,597   7,413   7,736   4,601

21. 1,865   8,387   1,119   5,413

22. 6,274   9,052   5,465   2,416

23. 5,222   1,942   5,861   9,249

24. 9,191   8,961   3,807   7,593

25. 1,957   5,030   7,144   7,244

26. 8,267   6,254   6,921   7,929

27. 6,531   3,517   8,087   4,291

28. 5,600   8,803   8,762   1,857

29. 2,365   3,921   8,397   3,883

30. 9,930   1,686   5,928   5,676

31. 8,011   4,044   2,722   6,154

32. 7,663   2,714   9,178   6,097

33. 9,829   8,465   2,869   8,567

34. 1,269   1,492   6,333   5,610

35. 2,465 3,190 8,881 3,756

36. 1,965 2,173 6,815 6,418

37. 3,179 5,004 7,883 6,270

38. 1,563 9,923 7,663 1,271

39. 9,102 2,467 9,233 5,223

40. 4,532 1,767 1,265 4,816

41. 4,339 2,989 4,462 7,135

42. 6,934 1,195 1,587 1,873

43. 7,587 3,787 2,417 7,739

44. 2,804 3,171 4,710 6,837

45. 7,229 6,303 3,974 3,659

46. 4,830 3,907 5,533 9,905

47. 1,802 2,598 9,464 8,801

48. 2,258 2,110 2,077 1,698

49. 2,924 5,065 9,417 8,976

50. 7,711 9,679 9,483 2,984

Circle the Numbers

Circle the even numbers in each group.

1. 4,416   7,010   8,682   7,776
2. (8,506)   9,923   (8,466)   6,931

3. 7,756   3,396   7,994   8,228
4. 7,792   7,606   9,985   1,431

5. 7,455   4,557   6,333   5,336
6. 1,730   2,785   9,614   6,477

7. 2,709   1,719   5,814   7,739
8. 3,753   5,734   9,126   7,549

9. 6,820   1,990   9,242   7,819
10. 5,224   7,756   2,399   1,878

11. 4,131   3,532   2,044   8,862
12. 4,116   3,849   3,906   5,318

13. 5,080   8,985   2,520   4,154
14. 4,346   5,147   2,253   2,630

15. 7,396   3,205   6,067   7,787
16. 5,109   1,727   4,177   3,022

17. 4,270   1,444   2,408   6,802

18. 8,364   3,165   6,206   9,699

19. 3,158   5,455   2,204   8,197

20. 1,741   1,752   3,361   8,859

21. 7,812   1,496   3,658   4,767

22. 4,214   5,971   4,202   2,673

23. 9,736   7,611   1,423   3,019

24. 2,689   4,611   6,769   3,404

25. 9,354   9,022   5,591   3,671

26. 2,441   7,103   6,954   2,914

27. 3,778   2,821   1,996   8,891

28. 3,942   4,056   1,889   6,644

29. 9,843   7,207   9,974   4,612

30. 8,068   9,410   8,808   8,298

31. 7,241   9,735   7,066   1,752

32. 2,741   4,187   8,009   8,546

33. 8,685   8,800   8,843   2,718

34. 6,160   9,690   7,418   1,708

35. 4,542 1,744 1,988 2,392   **36.** 4,975 5,311 8,730 6,680

37. 6,721 4,779 3,175 5,481   **38.** 4,637 3,156 5,335 9,944

39. 1,213 7,293 6,430 2,705   **40.** 1,037 6,201 1,172 9,591

41. 4,811 3,449 1,205 5,141   **42.** 5,213 9,170 1,483 1,153

43. 9,789 9,265 1,070 7,324   **44.** 8,421 7,415 4,322 2,930

45. 2,004 1,385 5,030 7,962   **46.** 2,011 3,528 4,908 6,529

47. 4,464 8,898 2,505 8,866   **48.** 4,259 5,712 1,670 8,340

49. 1,571 2,397 7,581 2,525   **50.** 5,105 4,589 2,467 7,551

Missing Numbers: Before and After

1. _7,498_ 7,499 _7,500_

2. ______ 8,735 ______

3. ______ 8,663 ______

4. ______ 7,711 ______

5. ______ 5,946 ______

6. ______ 2,910 ______

7. ______ 5,289 ______

Missing Numbers: Between

1. 4,292 _4293_ 4,294

2. 5,687 ______ 5,689

3. 3,084 ______ 3,086

4. 2,522 ______ 2,524

5. 3,968 ______ 3,970

6. 1,700 ______ 1,702

7. 2,169 ______ 2,171

8. __________ 7,743 __________

8. 8,572 __________ 8,574

9. __________ 3,083 __________

9. 8,533 __________ 8,535

10. __________ 2,414 __________

10. 1,675 __________ 1,677

11. __________ 9,529 __________

11. 7,658 __________ 7,660

12. __________ 1,560 __________

12. 6,887 __________ 6,889

13. __________ 8,858 __________

13. 8,587 __________ 8,589

14. __________ 6,485 __________

14. 6,747 __________ 6,749

15. __________ 1,642 __________

15. 9,825 __________ 9,827

16. _______ 8,398 _______

16. 7,817 _______ 7,819

17. _______ 6,701 _______

17. 8,910 _______ 8,912

18. _______ 3,480 _______

18. 4,662 _______ 4,664

19. _______ 6,098 _______

19. 7,829 _______ 7,831

20. _______ 7,150 _______

20. 4,439 _______ 4,441

21. _______ 8,957 _______

21. 7,368 _______ 7,370

22. _______ 8,922 _______

22. 5,890 _______ 5,892

23. _______ 2,649 _______

23. 5,007 _______ 5,009

24.	_______ 7,042 _______		**24.** 7,163 _______ 7,165	
25.	_______ 8,573 _______		**25.** 3,814 _______ 3,816	
26.	_______ 2,722 _______		**26.** 3,981 _______ 3,983	
27.	_______ 1,906 _______		**27.** 3,909 _______ 3,911	
28.	_______ 4,731 _______		**28.** 9,876 _______ 9,878	
29.	_______ 5,065 _______		**29.** 6,123 _______ 6,125	
30.	_______ 5,193 _______		**30.** 6,771 _______ 6,773	
31.	_______ 4,663 _______		**31.** 2,256 _______ 2,258	

32. _____ 3,317 _____   **32.** 3,960 _____ 3,962

33. _____ 3,816 _____   **33.** 6,669 _____ 6,671

34. _____ 7,017 _____   **34.** 1,732 _____ 1,734

35. _____ 8,836 _____   **35.** 8,536 _____ 8,538

36. _____ 3,434 _____   **36.** 4,443 _____ 4,445

37. _____ 7,822 _____   **37.** 1,232 _____ 1,234

38. _____ 2,475 _____   **38.** 8,932 _____ 8,934

39. _____ 3,942 _____   **39.** 6,715 _____ 6,717

40. _________ 1,039 _________

41. _________ 2,656 _________

42. _________ 9,329 _________

43. _________ 7,524 _________

44. _________ 4,068 _________

45. _________ 1,588 _________

46. _________ 2,998 _________

47. _________ 8,956 _________

40. 1,064 _________ 1,066

41. 5,554 _________ 5,556

42. 4,202 _________ 4,204

43. 8,803 _________ 8,805

44. 4,498 _________ 4,500

45. 7,587 _________ 7,589

46. 3,858 _________ 3,860

47. 3,756 _________ 3,758

48. 2,745   **48.** 5,191   5,193

49. 1,754   **49.** 5,738   5,740

50. 2,640   **50.** 4,081   4,083

51. 8,556   **51.** 1,284   1,286

52. 1,430   **52.** 9,807   9,809

53. 1,394   **53.** 2,849   2,851

54. 9,149   **54.** 1,196   1,198

55. 4,476   **55.** 7,206   7,208

56. _______ 2,696 _______   **56.** 5,953 _______ 5,955

57. _______ 7,010 _______   **57.** 1,551 _______ 1,553

58. _______ 8,311 _______   **58.** 5,792 _______ 5,794

59. _______ 1,482 _______   **59.** 2,292 _______ 2,294

60. _______ 9,177 _______   **60.** 3,360 _______ 3,362

61. _______ 4,870 _______   **61.** 9,775 _______ 9,777

62. _______ 9,385 _______   **62.** 7,091 _______ 7,093

63. _______ 8,683 _______   **63.** 6,723 _______ 6,725

64.   9,979

64. 6,240   6,242

65.   4,262

65. 1,027   1,029

66.   5,706

66. 4,212   4,214

67.   4,465

67. 4,046   4,048

68.   5,730

68. 7,284   7,286

69.   6,790

69. 8,568   8,570

70.   7,421

70. 2,683   2,685

71.   3,279

71. 7,192   7,194

72. _____ 7,275 _____   **72.** 6,548 _____ 6,550

73. _____ 6,149 _____   **73.** 7,022 _____ 7,024

74. _____ 3,041 _____   **74.** 6,662 _____ 6,664

75. _____ 8,873 _____   **75.** 8,281 _____ 8,283

76. _____ 8,666 _____   **76.** 1,580 _____ 1,582

77. _____ 4,046 _____   **77.** 2,356 _____ 2,358

78. _____ 9,843 _____   **78.** 1,940 _____ 1,942

79. _____ 7,686 _____   **79.** 6,375 _____ 6,377

Double Digit Addition

Find the Sum.

1.
```
   91
+  69
------
  160
```

2.
```
   38
+  84
------
```

3.
```
   26
+  21
------
```

4.
```
   35
+  20
------
```

5.
```
   54
+  17
------
```

6.
```
   61
+  37
------
```

7.
```
   16
+  90
------
```

8.
```
   80
+  54
------
```

9.
```
   90
+  66
------
```

10.
```
   89
+  70
------
```

11.
```
   58
+  56
------
```

12.
```
   23
+  29
------
```

13.
```
   27
+  89
------
```

14.
```
   46
+  94
------
```

15.
```
   76
+  42
------
```

16.
```
   64
+  34
------
```

17.
```
   78
+  73
------
```

18.
```
   32
+  14
------
```

19.
```
   19
+  47
------
```

20.
```
   65
+  61
------
```

21.
```
   97
+  51
------
```

22.
```
   85
+  23
------
```

23.
```
   28
+  61
------
```

24.
```
   46
+  95
------
```

25.
```
   81
+  85
------
```

26. 21 + 41	**27.** 43 + 16	**28.** 46 + 45	**29.** 56 + 19	**30.** 67 + 36
31. 74 + 41	**32.** 43 + 23	**33.** 52 + 37	**34.** 58 + 43	**35.** 68 + 76
36. 45 + 53	**37.** 12 + 38	**38.** 72 + 17	**39.** 70 + 99	**40.** 11 + 66
41. 53 + 50	**42.** 23 + 90	**43.** 30 + 33	**44.** 91 + 72	**45.** 37 + 86
46. 57 + 10	**47.** 79 + 38	**48.** 86 + 66	**49.** 19 + 72	**50.** 71 + 90

51.	52.	53.	54.	55.
13 + 13	38 + 15	50 + 67	39 + 14	43 + 39

56.	57.	58.	59.	60.
74 + 56	18 + 11	83 + 34	28 + 52	91 + 28

61.	62.	63.	64.	65.
46 + 85	15 + 81	29 + 44	72 + 72	52 + 17

66.	67.	68.	69.	70.
97 + 97	38 + 19	62 + 49	22 + 18	49 + 62

71.	72.	73.	74.	75.
93 + 86	40 + 97	22 + 11	91 + 78	54 + 61

76. $\begin{array}{r} 48 \\ +\ 66 \\ \hline \end{array}$	**77.** $\begin{array}{r} 80 \\ +\ 53 \\ \hline \end{array}$	**78.** $\begin{array}{r} 55 \\ +\ 28 \\ \hline \end{array}$	**79.** $\begin{array}{r} 97 \\ +\ 56 \\ \hline \end{array}$	**80.** $\begin{array}{r} 85 \\ +\ 16 \\ \hline \end{array}$
81. $\begin{array}{r} 94 \\ +\ 66 \\ \hline \end{array}$	**82.** $\begin{array}{r} 62 \\ +\ 36 \\ \hline \end{array}$	**83.** $\begin{array}{r} 41 \\ +\ 75 \\ \hline \end{array}$	**84.** $\begin{array}{r} 28 \\ +\ 98 \\ \hline \end{array}$	**85.** $\begin{array}{r} 48 \\ +\ 44 \\ \hline \end{array}$
86. $\begin{array}{r} 22 \\ +\ 20 \\ \hline \end{array}$	**87.** $\begin{array}{r} 13 \\ +\ 39 \\ \hline \end{array}$	**88.** $\begin{array}{r} 35 \\ +\ 58 \\ \hline \end{array}$	**89.** $\begin{array}{r} 55 \\ +\ 17 \\ \hline \end{array}$	**90.** $\begin{array}{r} 69 \\ +\ 28 \\ \hline \end{array}$
91. $\begin{array}{r} 52 \\ +\ 93 \\ \hline \end{array}$	**92.** $\begin{array}{r} 28 \\ +\ 89 \\ \hline \end{array}$	**93.** $\begin{array}{r} 68 \\ +\ 41 \\ \hline \end{array}$	**94.** $\begin{array}{r} 28 \\ +\ 84 \\ \hline \end{array}$	**95.** $\begin{array}{r} 63 \\ +\ 45 \\ \hline \end{array}$
96. $\begin{array}{r} 51 \\ +\ 65 \\ \hline \end{array}$	**97.** $\begin{array}{r} 32 \\ +\ 43 \\ \hline \end{array}$	**98.** $\begin{array}{r} 67 \\ +\ 37 \\ \hline \end{array}$	**99.** $\begin{array}{r} 35 \\ +\ 14 \\ \hline \end{array}$	**100.** $\begin{array}{r} 66 \\ +\ 45 \\ \hline \end{array}$

Three-Digit Addition

Find the Sum.

1. $\begin{array}{r} 820 \\ +\ 933 \\ \hline 1{,}753 \end{array}$	**2.** $\begin{array}{r} 407 \\ +\ 208 \\ \hline \end{array}$	**3.** $\begin{array}{r} 499 \\ +\ 376 \\ \hline \end{array}$

4. $\begin{array}{r} 638 \\ +\ 510 \\ \hline \end{array}$ **5.** $\begin{array}{r} 282 \\ +\ 964 \\ \hline \end{array}$

6. $\begin{array}{r} 721 \\ +\ 907 \\ \hline \end{array}$ **7.** $\begin{array}{r} 868 \\ +\ 670 \\ \hline \end{array}$ **8.** $\begin{array}{r} 639 \\ +\ 107 \\ \hline \end{array}$ **9.** $\begin{array}{r} 482 \\ +\ 717 \\ \hline \end{array}$ **10.** $\begin{array}{r} 673 \\ +\ 996 \\ \hline \end{array}$

11. $\begin{array}{r} 582 \\ +\ 433 \\ \hline \end{array}$ **12.** $\begin{array}{r} 450 \\ +\ 131 \\ \hline \end{array}$ **13.** $\begin{array}{r} 923 \\ +\ 560 \\ \hline \end{array}$ **14.** $\begin{array}{r} 883 \\ +\ 690 \\ \hline \end{array}$ **15.** $\begin{array}{r} 715 \\ +\ 976 \\ \hline \end{array}$

16. $\begin{array}{r} 338 \\ +\ 519 \\ \hline \end{array}$ **17.** $\begin{array}{r} 501 \\ +\ 337 \\ \hline \end{array}$ **18.** $\begin{array}{r} 466 \\ +\ 589 \\ \hline \end{array}$ **19.** $\begin{array}{r} 634 \\ +\ 174 \\ \hline \end{array}$ **20.** $\begin{array}{r} 503 \\ +\ 411 \\ \hline \end{array}$

21. $\begin{array}{r} 776 \\ +\ 768 \\ \hline \end{array}$ **22.** $\begin{array}{r} 670 \\ +\ 673 \\ \hline \end{array}$ **23.** $\begin{array}{r} 729 \\ +\ 608 \\ \hline \end{array}$ **24.** $\begin{array}{r} 790 \\ +\ 650 \\ \hline \end{array}$ **25.** $\begin{array}{r} 795 \\ +\ 670 \\ \hline \end{array}$

26. 888 + 631	**27.** 463 + 672	**28.** 875 + 487	**29.** 583 + 376	**30.** 285 + 938
31. 492 + 948	**32.** 794 + 304	**33.** 726 + 302	**34.** 506 + 631	**35.** 305 + 149
36. 473 + 408	**37.** 314 + 362	**38.** 320 + 813	**39.** 762 + 775	**40.** 400 + 415
41. 770 + 333	**42.** 893 + 145	**43.** 189 + 706	**44.** 156 + 828	**45.** 461 + 978
46. 106 + 357	**47.** 888 + 564	**48.** 918 + 828	**49.** 973 + 465	**50.** 946 + 527

51.	52.	53.	54.	55.
201 + 258	445 + 746	297 + 580	417 + 201	452 + 161

56.	57.	58.	59.	60.
723 + 807	975 + 869	268 + 259	154 + 749	216 + 120

61.	62.	63.	64.	65.
246 + 677	270 + 326	143 + 215	518 + 749	442 + 492

66.	67.	68.	69.	70.
840 + 397	828 + 872	313 + 611	887 + 248	847 + 607

71.	72.	73.	74.	75.
389 + 955	476 + 400	355 + 298	382 + 119	396 + 760

76. 773 + 324	**77.** 350 + 926	**78.** 381 + 523	**79.** 987 + 219	**80.** 703 + 182
81. 162 + 667	**82.** 757 + 959	**83.** 321 + 426	**84.** 978 + 203	**85.** 656 + 656
86. 371 + 906	**87.** 901 + 607	**88.** 730 + 290	**89.** 301 + 869	**90.** 969 + 844
91. 833 + 499	**92.** 452 + 682	**93.** 717 + 616	**94.** 147 + 901	**95.** 591 + 789
96. 623 + 768	**97.** 544 + 765	**98.** 546 + 720	**99.** 298 + 516	**100.** 179 + 928

Double Digit Subtraction

Find the Difference.

1. 32
  − 14
  18

2. 46
  − 36

3. 49
  − 43

4. 42
  − 33

5. 29
  − 12

6. 32
  − 13

7. 25
  − 23

8. 35
  − 26

9. 31
  − 12

10. 34
  − 26

11. 38
  − 12

12. 61
  − 53

13. 13
  − 12

14. 46
  − 15

15. 16
  − 10

16. 98
  − 77

17. 78
  − 13

18. 62
  − 42

19. 14
  − 13

20. 29
  − 26

21.	22.	23.	24.	25.
29 − 16	70 − 37	56 − 31	61 − 43	51 − 46

26.	27.	28.	29.	30.
50 − 15	27 − 17	64 − 19	66 − 41	70 − 62

31.	32.	33.	34.	35.
50 − 18	67 − 22	20 − 15	42 − 14	33 − 25

36.	37.	38.	39.	40.
62 − 39	87 − 44	51 − 50	47 − 15	39 − 27

41.	42.	43.	44.	45.
97 − 75	71 − 22	60 − 53	61 − 28	49 − 27

46. $\begin{aligned} 98 \\ -\ 53 \\ \hline \end{aligned}$	**47.** $\begin{aligned} 11 \\ -\ 10 \\ \hline \end{aligned}$	**48.** $\begin{aligned} 44 \\ -\ 10 \\ \hline \end{aligned}$	**49.** $\begin{aligned} 72 \\ -\ 39 \\ \hline \end{aligned}$	**50.** $\begin{aligned} 40 \\ -\ 11 \\ \hline \end{aligned}$
51. $\begin{aligned} 18 \\ -\ 14 \\ \hline \end{aligned}$	**52.** $\begin{aligned} 45 \\ -\ 38 \\ \hline \end{aligned}$	**53.** $\begin{aligned} 35 \\ -\ 32 \\ \hline \end{aligned}$	**54.** $\begin{aligned} 34 \\ -\ 28 \\ \hline \end{aligned}$	**55.** $\begin{aligned} 96 \\ -\ 65 \\ \hline \end{aligned}$
56. $\begin{aligned} 76 \\ -\ 44 \\ \hline \end{aligned}$	**57.** $\begin{aligned} 30 \\ -\ 12 \\ \hline \end{aligned}$	**58.** $\begin{aligned} 89 \\ -\ 65 \\ \hline \end{aligned}$	**59.** $\begin{aligned} 68 \\ -\ 25 \\ \hline \end{aligned}$	**60.** $\begin{aligned} 92 \\ -\ 11 \\ \hline \end{aligned}$
61. $\begin{aligned} 71 \\ -\ 61 \\ \hline \end{aligned}$	**62.** $\begin{aligned} 70 \\ -\ 16 \\ \hline \end{aligned}$	**63.** $\begin{aligned} 59 \\ -\ 36 \\ \hline \end{aligned}$	**64.** $\begin{aligned} 15 \\ -\ 12 \\ \hline \end{aligned}$	**65.** $\begin{aligned} 35 \\ -\ 34 \\ \hline \end{aligned}$
66. $\begin{aligned} 80 \\ -\ 31 \\ \hline \end{aligned}$	**67.** $\begin{aligned} 55 \\ -\ 34 \\ \hline \end{aligned}$	**68.** $\begin{aligned} 42 \\ -\ 38 \\ \hline \end{aligned}$	**69.** $\begin{aligned} 91 \\ -\ 64 \\ \hline \end{aligned}$	**70.** $\begin{aligned} 62 \\ -\ 52 \\ \hline \end{aligned}$

71.	72.	73.	74.	75.
71 − 39	34 − 32	50 − 37	54 − 21	83 − 16

76.	77.	78.	79.	80.
20 − 11	79 − 49	21 − 12	40 − 32	73 − 43

81.	82.	83.	84.	85.
42 − 36	74 − 69	62 − 29	40 − 29	58 − 57

86.	87.	88.	89.	90.
69 − 16	66 − 60	24 − 13	84 − 57	17 − 13

91.	92.	93.	94.	95.
95 − 13	22 − 18	26 − 17	77 − 64	77 − 58

Three-Digit Subtraction

Find the Difference.

| 1. | 394
− 350
44 | 2. | 196
− 184 | 3. | 490
− 444 | 4. | 778
− 332 | 5. | 400
− 123 |

| 6. | 407
− 363 | 7. | 737
− 634 | 8. | 478
− 104 | 9. | 500
− 454 | 10. | 464
− 438 |

| 11. | 424
− 329 | 12. | 689
− 296 | 13. | 605
− 266 | 14. | 701
− 111 | 15. | 770
− 203 |

| 16. | 656
− 401 | 17. | 890
− 745 | 18. | 687
− 576 | 19. | 101
− 101 | 20. | 508
− 210 |

21. 500 − 295	**22.** 370 − 101	**23.** 126 − 103	**24.** 391 − 185	**25.** 354 − 143
26. 987 − 868	**27.** 455 − 394	**28.** 425 − 302	**29.** 277 − 237	**30.** 379 − 129
31. 293 − 242	**32.** 636 − 196	**33.** 513 − 430	**34.** 979 − 885	**35.** 266 − 201
36. 108 − 106	**37.** 487 − 152	**38.** 536 − 480	**39.** 465 − 338	**40.** 374 − 227
41. 105 − 102	**42.** 762 − 481	**43.** 250 − 213	**44.** 232 − 107	**45.** 509 − 113

46.	47.	48.	49.	50.
653 − 226	499 − 239	150 − 135	901 − 197	590 − 213

51.	52.	53.	54.	55.
208 − 147	196 − 165	245 − 143	491 − 202	408 − 251

56.	57.	58.	59.	60.
294 − 206	521 − 457	190 − 175	998 − 120	112 − 108

61.	62.	63.	64.	65.
686 − 643	494 − 160	994 − 799	323 − 118	170 − 154

66.	67.	68.	69.	70.
982 − 351	196 − 107	408 − 277	343 − 115	472 − 424

Mixed Two-Digit Practice

Addition and Subtraction

1.
```
   569
 + 389
 -----
   958
```

2.
```
   396
 - 340
 -----
```

3.
```
   164
 - 110
 -----
```

4.
```
   609
 - 508
 -----
```

5.
```
   550
 + 457
 -----
```

6.
```
   777
 + 252
 -----
```

7.
```
   906
 + 419
 -----
```

8.
```
   938
 - 329
 -----
```

9.
```
   599
 - 361
 -----
```

10.
```
   250
 - 247
 -----
```

11.
```
   629
 - 115
 -----
```

12.
```
   345
 - 206
 -----
```

13.
```
   560
 - 373
 -----
```

14.
```
   949
 + 327
 -----
```

15.
```
   596
 + 616
 -----
```

16.
```
   204
 - 127
 -----
```

17. $\begin{array}{r} 600 \\ -\ 548 \\ \hline \end{array}$	**18.** $\begin{array}{r} 856 \\ -\ 326 \\ \hline \end{array}$	**19.** $\begin{array}{r} 809 \\ -\ 634 \\ \hline \end{array}$	**20.** $\begin{array}{r} 131 \\ -\ 102 \\ \hline \end{array}$
21. $\begin{array}{r} 387 \\ +\ 484 \\ \hline \end{array}$	**22.** $\begin{array}{r} 154 \\ +\ 168 \\ \hline \end{array}$	**23.** $\begin{array}{r} 114 \\ +\ 502 \\ \hline \end{array}$	**24.** $\begin{array}{r} 519 \\ -\ 330 \\ \hline \end{array}$
25. $\begin{array}{r} 363 \\ +\ 691 \\ \hline \end{array}$	**26.** $\begin{array}{r} 872 \\ -\ 588 \\ \hline \end{array}$	**27.** $\begin{array}{r} 558 \\ -\ 107 \\ \hline \end{array}$	**28.** $\begin{array}{r} 175 \\ -\ 122 \\ \hline \end{array}$
29. $\begin{array}{r} 222 \\ -\ 147 \\ \hline \end{array}$	**30.** $\begin{array}{r} 603 \\ +\ 198 \\ \hline \end{array}$	**31.** $\begin{array}{r} 289 \\ +\ 363 \\ \hline \end{array}$	**32.** $\begin{array}{r} 864 \\ +\ 291 \\ \hline \end{array}$
33. $\begin{array}{r} 976 \\ -\ 577 \\ \hline \end{array}$	**34.** $\begin{array}{r} 352 \\ -\ 329 \\ \hline \end{array}$	**35.** $\begin{array}{r} 395 \\ -\ 110 \\ \hline \end{array}$	**36.** $\begin{array}{r} 779 \\ -\ 725 \\ \hline \end{array}$

37. 839 + 716	**38.** 374 − 362	**39.** 463 − 463	**40.** 256 + 154
41. 725 + 666	**42.** 500 − 388	**43.** 742 − 700	**44.** 339 − 204
45. 973 − 774	**46.** 708 + 483	**47.** 497 + 445	**48.** 677 + 153
49. 437 − 374	**50.** 790 − 690	**51.** 221 + 516	**52.** 825 − 105
53. 521 + 763	**54.** 698 − 420	**55.** 801 + 458	**56.** 299 + 717

57. 681 + 118	**58.** 777 + 909	**59.** 520 − 340	**60.** 554 + 255
61. 516 + 729	**62.** 853 + 471	**63.** 200 + 286	**64.** 950 − 927
65. 592 + 586	**66.** 412 + 291	**67.** 368 − 134	**68.** 263 + 894
69. 600 + 930	**70.** 907 + 903	**71.** 657 − 418	**72.** 986 + 708
73. 490 + 960	**74.** 382 + 846	**75.** 977 − 667	**76.** 271 + 839

Addition with Regrouping

Find the sum.

1. 611 + 899 1,510	**2.** 588 + 888	**3.** 513 + 997	**4.** 715 + 597
5. 193 + 928	**6.** 926 + 687	**7.** 774 + 686	**8.** 395 + 927
9. 119 + 994	**10.** 799 + 482	**11.** 192 + 989	**12.** 431 + 799
13. 517 + 798	**14.** 119 + 997	**15.** 731 + 389	**16.** 191 + 929

17. $\begin{array}{r} 962 \\ +\ 658 \\ \hline \end{array}$	**18.** $\begin{array}{r} 879 \\ +\ 247 \\ \hline \end{array}$	**19.** $\begin{array}{r} 316 \\ +\ 795 \\ \hline \end{array}$	**20.** $\begin{array}{r} 429 \\ +\ 799 \\ \hline \end{array}$
21. $\begin{array}{r} 263 \\ +\ 849 \\ \hline \end{array}$	**22.** $\begin{array}{r} 912 \\ +\ 598 \\ \hline \end{array}$	**23.** $\begin{array}{r} 654 \\ +\ 987 \\ \hline \end{array}$	**24.** $\begin{array}{r} 839 \\ +\ 376 \\ \hline \end{array}$
25. $\begin{array}{r} 681 \\ +\ 949 \\ \hline \end{array}$	**26.** $\begin{array}{r} 215 \\ +\ 896 \\ \hline \end{array}$	**27.** $\begin{array}{r} 814 \\ +\ 599 \\ \hline \end{array}$	**28.** $\begin{array}{r} 589 \\ +\ 521 \\ \hline \end{array}$
29. $\begin{array}{r} 496 \\ +\ 889 \\ \hline \end{array}$	**30.** $\begin{array}{r} 473 \\ +\ 747 \\ \hline \end{array}$	**31.** $\begin{array}{r} 161 \\ +\ 989 \\ \hline \end{array}$	**32.** $\begin{array}{r} 789 \\ +\ 877 \\ \hline \end{array}$
33. $\begin{array}{r} 135 \\ +\ 997 \\ \hline \end{array}$	**34.** $\begin{array}{r} 655 \\ +\ 498 \\ \hline \end{array}$	**35.** $\begin{array}{r} 814 \\ +\ 298 \\ \hline \end{array}$	**36.** $\begin{array}{r} 221 \\ +\ 989 \\ \hline \end{array}$

37. $\begin{array}{r} 815 \\ +\ 499 \\ \hline \end{array}$	**38.** $\begin{array}{r} 319 \\ +\ 797 \\ \hline \end{array}$	**39.** $\begin{array}{r} 476 \\ +\ 856 \\ \hline \end{array}$	**40.** $\begin{array}{r} 644 \\ +\ 678 \\ \hline \end{array}$
41. $\begin{array}{r} 918 \\ +\ 792 \\ \hline \end{array}$	**42.** $\begin{array}{r} 817 \\ +\ 799 \\ \hline \end{array}$	**43.** $\begin{array}{r} 281 \\ +\ 979 \\ \hline \end{array}$	**44.** $\begin{array}{r} 414 \\ +\ 897 \\ \hline \end{array}$
45. $\begin{array}{r} 167 \\ +\ 958 \\ \hline \end{array}$	**46.** $\begin{array}{r} 751 \\ +\ 969 \\ \hline \end{array}$	**47.** $\begin{array}{r} 182 \\ +\ 988 \\ \hline \end{array}$	**48.** $\begin{array}{r} 658 \\ +\ 964 \\ \hline \end{array}$
49. $\begin{array}{r} 615 \\ +\ 495 \\ \hline \end{array}$	**50.** $\begin{array}{r} 539 \\ +\ 896 \\ \hline \end{array}$	**51.** $\begin{array}{r} 348 \\ +\ 776 \\ \hline \end{array}$	**52.** $\begin{array}{r} 561 \\ +\ 569 \\ \hline \end{array}$
53. $\begin{array}{r} 819 \\ +\ 691 \\ \hline \end{array}$	**54.** $\begin{array}{r} 697 \\ +\ 734 \\ \hline \end{array}$	**55.** $\begin{array}{r} 375 \\ +\ 866 \\ \hline \end{array}$	**56.** $\begin{array}{r} 844 \\ +\ 698 \\ \hline \end{array}$

Subtraction with Regrouping

Find the difference.

1. 704 − 616 = 88	**2.** 803 − 349	**3.** 600 − 512	**4.** 606 − 387
5. 403 − 166	**6.** 201 − 115	**7.** 407 − 179	**8.** 400 − 143
9. 500 − 222	**10.** 201 − 135	**11.** 407 − 339	**12.** 306 − 148
13. 201 − 134	**14.** 908 − 579	**15.** 908 − 629	**16.** 202 − 113

17. 802 − 187

18. 201 − 124

19. 808 − 289

20. 503 − 338

21. 506 − 137

22. 402 − 127

23. 600 − 275

24. 204 − 149

25. 201 − 152

26. 304 − 197

27. 600 − 362

28. 301 − 297

29. 601 − 394

30. 207 − 119

31. 200 − 134

32. 407 − 348

33. 205 − 166

34. 403 − 196

35. 202 − 136

36. 300 − 141

37. $\begin{array}{r}808\\-\ 539\\\hline\end{array}$	**38.** $\begin{array}{r}703\\-\ 258\\\hline\end{array}$	**39.** $\begin{array}{r}404\\-\ 166\\\hline\end{array}$	**40.** $\begin{array}{r}605\\-\ 537\\\hline\end{array}$
41. $\begin{array}{r}301\\-\ 179\\\hline\end{array}$	**42.** $\begin{array}{r}407\\-\ 248\\\hline\end{array}$	**43.** $\begin{array}{r}404\\-\ 137\\\hline\end{array}$	**44.** $\begin{array}{r}703\\-\ 268\\\hline\end{array}$
45. $\begin{array}{r}808\\-\ 269\\\hline\end{array}$	**46.** $\begin{array}{r}608\\-\ 239\\\hline\end{array}$	**47.** $\begin{array}{r}203\\-\ 134\\\hline\end{array}$	**48.** $\begin{array}{r}504\\-\ 315\\\hline\end{array}$
49. $\begin{array}{r}703\\-\ 488\\\hline\end{array}$	**50.** $\begin{array}{r}903\\-\ 825\\\hline\end{array}$	**51.** $\begin{array}{r}908\\-\ 689\\\hline\end{array}$	**52.** $\begin{array}{r}503\\-\ 116\\\hline\end{array}$
53. $\begin{array}{r}308\\-\ 219\\\hline\end{array}$	**54.** $\begin{array}{r}706\\-\ 699\\\hline\end{array}$	**55.** $\begin{array}{r}601\\-\ 276\\\hline\end{array}$	**56.** $\begin{array}{r}201\\-\ 174\\\hline\end{array}$

57.	58.	59.	60.
803 − 557	600 − 581	408 − 149	202 − 133

61.	62.	63.	64.
405 − 346	506 − 117	207 − 158	601 − 462

65.	66.	67.	68.
301 − 243	804 − 486	807 − 359	305 − 177

69.	70.	71.	72.
900 − 686	502 − 469	601 − 258	301 − 264

73.	74.	75.	76.
503 − 466	906 − 678	308 − 299	802 − 715

Double Digit Three-Addends

Find the sum.

1.
```
   35
   76
 + 56
 ____
  167
```

2.
```
   26
   95
 + 71
 ____
```

3.
```
   89
   56
 + 45
 ____
```

4.
```
   89
   18
 + 36
 ____
```

5.
```
   48
   40
 + 80
 ____
```

6.
```
   32
   74
 + 11
 ____
```

7.
```
   17
   39
 + 62
 ____
```

8.
```
   58
   24
 + 27
 ____
```

9.
```
   80
   34
 + 14
 ____
```

10.
```
   26
   39
 + 89
 ____
```

11.
```
   51
   37
 + 90
 ____
```

12.
```
   99
   34
 + 20
 ____
```

13. 85 15 $+\ 47$	**14.** 31 85 $+\ 10$	**15.** 55 77 $+\ 30$	**16.** 96 44 $+\ 20$
17. 20 69 $+\ 98$	**18.** 32 88 $+\ 54$	**19.** 36 75 $+\ 62$	**20.** 39 45 $+\ 71$
21. 67 73 $+\ 27$	**22.** 55 47 $+\ 81$	**23.** 45 48 $+\ 16$	**24.** 70 46 $+\ 69$
25. 63 85 $+\ 53$	**26.** 62 14 $+\ 47$	**27.** 96 83 $+\ 89$	**28.** 93 16 $+\ 68$

29. 90 30 + 48	**30.** 46 73 + 57	**31.** 58 56 + 69	**32.** 75 63 + 21
33. 82 98 + 40	**34.** 48 61 + 95	**35.** 14 49 + 33	**36.** 39 68 + 13
37. 11 73 + 72	**38.** 25 42 + 62	**39.** 81 74 + 67	**40.** 58 65 + 28
41. 43 98 + 75	**42.** 57 22 + 89	**43.** 99 87 + 32	**44.** 42 79 + 14

45.	46.	47.	48.
17 58 + 31	93 88 + 66	45 61 + 61	45 46 + 10

49.	50.	51.	52.
85 43 + 24	18 94 + 88	53 34 + 44	22 15 + 63

53.	54.	55.	56.
30 56 + 36	43 39 + 80	80 68 + 93	67 18 + 82

57.	58.	59.	60.
40 87 + 84	11 23 + 14	65 97 + 62	74 72 + 79

61.	**62.**	**63.**	**64.**
75 91 + 92	43 87 + 55	69 94 + 53	68 73 + 42

65.	**66.**	**67.**	**68.**
40 13 + 31	80 64 + 77	17 27 + 35	41 76 + 17

69.	**70.**	**71.**	**72.**
14 53 + 21	40 55 + 17	10 55 + 83	57 67 + 48

73.	**74.**	**75.**	**76.**
87 47 + 80	47 97 + 23	40 72 + 24	52 70 + 20

77.
```
   82
   84
+  43
______
```

78.
```
   85
   68
+  54
______
```

79.
```
   54
   44
+  24
______
```

80.
```
   84
   38
+  45
______
```

81.
```
   44
   40
+  49
______
```

82.
```
   45
   67
+  28
______
```

83.
```
   58
   82
+  45
______
```

84.
```
   83
   92
+  26
______
```

85.
```
   96
   68
+  29
______
```

86.
```
   22
   11
+  15
______
```

87.
```
   92
   61
+  82
______
```

88.
```
   11
   57
+  70
______
```

89.
```
   73
   25
+  86
______
```

90.
```
   39
   12
+  32
______
```

91.
```
   33
   13
+  19
______
```

92.
```
   45
   14
+  68
______
```

Can you Make 1000?

Find the numbers.

1. 14 + 986 = 1,000

2. 24 + ___ = 1,000

3. 8 + ___ = 1,000

4. 4 + ___ = 1,000

5. 7 + ___ = 1,000

6. 38 + ___ = 1,000

7. 2 + ___ = 1,000

8. 16 + ___ = 1,000

9. 18 + ___ = 1,000

10. 19 + ___ = 1,000

11. 27 + ___ = 1,000

12. 12 + ___ = 1,000

13. 34 + ___ = 1,000

14. 6 + ___ = 1,000

15. 30 + ___ = 1,000

16. 9 + ___ = 1,000

17. $37 + \underline{\quad} = 1,000$

18. $3 + \underline{\quad} = 1,000$

19. $11 + \underline{\quad} = 1,000$

20. $5 + \underline{\quad} = 1,000$

21. $29 + \underline{\quad} = 1,000$

22. $28 + \underline{\quad} = 1,000$

23. $17 + \underline{\quad} = 1,000$

24. $39 + \underline{\quad} = 1,000$

25. $15 + \underline{\quad} = 1,000$

26. $35 + \underline{\quad} = 1,000$

27. $32 + \underline{\quad} = 1,000$

28. $22 + \underline{\quad} = 1,000$

29. $20 + \underline{\quad} = 1,000$

30. $10 + \underline{\quad} = 1,000$

31. $36 + \underline{\quad} = 1,000$

32. $13 + \underline{\quad} = 1,000$

33. $40 + \underline{\quad} = 1,000$

34. $33 + \underline{\quad} = 1,000$

35. $21 + \underline{\quad} = 1,000$

36. $31 + \underline{\quad} = 1,000$

Place Value

Determine the place value of the underlined digit.

1. 6,172 = **6 thousands**

2. 2,600 =

3. 9,334 =

4. 8,303 =

5. 2,083 =

6. 4,959 =

7. 4,360 =

8. 6,294 =

9. 6,759 =

10. 6,131 =

11. 7,646 =

12. 1,362 =

13. 8,847 =

14. 2,125 =

15. 4,712 =

16. 8,856 =

17. 6,8<u>4</u>4 = _________________

18. <u>6</u>,258 = _________________

19. 9,<u>2</u>62 = _________________

20. 2,39<u>5</u> = _________________

21. <u>1</u>,877 = _________________

22. 7,95<u>7</u> = _________________

23. 5,48<u>3</u> = _________________

24. <u>1</u>,872 = _________________

25. <u>7</u>,143 = _________________

26. <u>2</u>,160 = _________________

27. <u>8</u>,768 = _________________

28. <u>1</u>,610 = _________________

29. 5,6<u>0</u>5 = _________________

30. 3,0<u>2</u>9 = _________________

31. 3,5<u>8</u>0 = _________________

32. <u>5</u>,583 = _________________

33. 2,05<u>5</u> = _________________

34. 4,<u>3</u>58 = _________________

35. 9,390 = ___________

36. 6,287 = ___________

37. 2,356 = ___________

38. 5,782 = ___________

39. 1,925 = ___________

40. 7,549 = ___________

41. 6,905 = ___________

42. 2,661 = ___________

43. 6,390 = ___________

44. 5,703 = ___________

45. 2,294 = ___________

46. 6,567 = ___________

47. 9,786 = ___________

48. 8,579 = ___________

49. 9,051 = ___________

50. 4,692 = ___________

51. 6,223 = ___________

52. 1,408 = ___________

Place Value: Expanded Notation

Provide the expanded notation for each value.

1. 1583 _______________ one thousand five hundred eighty-three

2. _______________ eight thousand five hundred forty-eight

3. _______________ six thousand two

4. _______________ two thousand one hundred ninety-one

5. _______________ nine thousand seven hundred seventy-five

6. _______________ seven thousand nine hundred twenty-four

7. _______________ one thousand three hundred seventy-eight

8. _______________ eight thousand seven hundred twenty

9. _______________ two thousand seven hundred twenty-one

10. _______________ eight thousand two hundred nineteen

11. _______________ one thousand five hundred fifty-eight

12. _______________ nine thousand two hundred fifty-two

13. _______________ four thousand six hundred six

14. _______________ seven thousand four hundred thirty-nine

15. _______________ four thousand three hundred twenty-nine

16. _______________ one thousand three hundred fifty-four

17. _______________ two thousand three hundred thirty-three

18. _______________ eight thousand two hundred forty-four

19. _______________ nine thousand nine hundred five

20. _______________ seven thousand six hundred twenty-seven

21. _______________ one thousand three hundred forty-six

22. _______________ four thousand three hundred fifteen

23. _______________ seven thousand seventy-five

24. _______________ four thousand three hundred forty-two

25. _______________ one thousand nine hundred thirty-one

26. _______________ four thousand seven hundred twenty-two

27. _______________ two thousand six hundred forty-five

28. _______________ seven thousand ninety-seven

29. _______________ four thousand eight hundred thirteen

30. _______________ eight thousand six hundred four

31. _______________ nine thousand three hundred ninety-six

32. _______________ five thousand five hundred twenty-seven

33. _______________ two thousand eight hundred thirty-three

34. _______________ five thousand ten

35. _______________ four thousand thirty-nine

36. _______________ three thousand four hundred fifty-four

37. _______________ six thousand three hundred fifty-seven

38. _______________ two thousand nine hundred sixty-four

39. _______________ two thousand one hundred ninety-five

40. _______________ four thousand seven hundred thirty-five

41. _______________ two thousand seven hundred seventy-four

42. _______________ one thousand five hundred eleven

43. _______________ five thousand five hundred thirty-nine

44. _______________ seven thousand seventy-seven

45. ____________ six thousand two hundred eighty-seven

46. ____________ two thousand three hundred seventy-four

47. ____________ three thousand five hundred eighty-four

48. ____________ seven thousand seven hundred twenty-one

49. ____________ two thousand seven hundred forty-five

50. ____________ nine thousand one hundred seventy-four

51. ____________ seven thousand six hundred forty-seven

52. ____________ nine thousand six hundred twenty-six

53. ____________ six thousand seven hundred forty-one

54. __________   nine thousand seven hundred nine

55. __________   eight thousand five hundred thirty-seven

56. __________   seven thousand two hundred sixty-seven

57. __________   two thousand four hundred seventy-four

58. __________   two thousand six hundred sixty

59. __________   one thousand two hundred sixty

60. __________   six thousand fifty-four

61. __________   six thousand two hundred seventy-nine

Addition and Subtraction Quiz

1. What is 941 - 113 _____
    A. 829
    B. 827
    C. 828
    D. 830

2. What is 313 + 929 _____
    A. 1241
    B. 1242
    C. 1243
    D. 1244

3. What is 726 - 398 _____
    A. 327
    B. 328
    C. 329
    D. 330

4. What is 389 + 692 _____
    A. 1083
    B. 1080
    C. 1081
    D. 1082

5. What is 127 - 573 _____
    A. -444
    B. -447
    C. -446
    D. -445

6. What is 784 - 294 _____
    A. 490
    B. 489
    C. 491
    D. 492

7. What is 866 - 485 _____
    A. 380
    B. 381
    C. 383
    D. 382

8. What is 916 - 392 _____
    A. 525
    B. 526
    C. 523
    D. 524

9. What is 126 + 159 _______

    A. 287

    B. 285

    C. 286

    D. 284

10. What is 496 - 180 _______

    A. 316

    B. 318

    C. 317

    D. 315

11. What is 854 + 656 _______

    A. 1512

    B. 1511

    C. 1509

    D. 1510

12. What is 128 + 811 _______

    A. 940

    B. 941

    C. 939

    D. 938

13. What is 780 + 940 _______

    A. 1719

    B. 1720

    C. 1721

    D. 1722

14. What is 809 - 369 _______

    A. 442

    B. 441

    C. 440

    D. 439

15. What is 458 + 478 _______

    A. 936

    B. 937

    C. 935

    D. 938

16. What is 623 - 809 _______

    A. -186

    B. -185

    C. -184

    D. -187

17. What is 661 + 799 _____

A. 1460

B. 1459

C. 1462

D. 1461

18. What is 560 + 161 _____

A. 721

B. 723

C. 720

D. 722

19. What is 249 - 452 _____

A. -204

B. -201

C. -202

D. -203

20. What is 363 + 421 _____

A. 783

B. 785

C. 784

D. 786

21. What is 202 - 815 _____

A. -614

B. -613

C. -611

D. -612

22. What is 367 - 369 _____

A. -1

B. -3

C. -2

D. 0

23. What is 719 - 270 _____

A. 448

B. 451

C. 450

D. 449

24. What is 127 + 740 _____

A. 868

B. 867

C. 866

D. 869

25. What is 795 + 711 _____
    A. 1508
    B. 1507
    C. 1505
    D. 1506

26. What is 271 - 797 _____
    A. -527
    B. -526
    C. -524
    D. -525

27. What is 545 - 857 _____
    A. -311
    B. -310
    C. -313
    D. -312

28. What is 600 + 972 _____
    A. 1572
    B. 1573
    C. 1571
    D. 1574

29. What is 960 + 948 _____
    A. 1910
    B. 1909
    C. 1908
    D. 1907

30. What is 298 - 383 _____
    A. -84
    B. -86
    C. -85
    D. -83

31. What is 170 + 831 _____
    A. 1000
    B. 1003
    C. 1002
    D. 1001

32. What is 673 + 617 _____
    A. 1290
    B. 1291
    C. 1289
    D. 1292

33. What is 216 - 473 _____
   A. -255
   B. -257
   C. -256
   D. -258

34. What is 779 - 884 _____
   A. -106
   B. -105
   C. -103
   D. -104

35. What is 759 - 894 _____
   A. -136
   B. -134
   C. -133
   D. -135

36. What is 917 + 932 _____
   A. 1849
   B. 1848
   C. 1850
   D. 1851

37. What is 823 - 897 _____
   A. -75
   B. -74
   C. -73
   D. -72

38. What is 231 + 973 _____
   A. 1205
   B. 1204
   C. 1206
   D. 1203

39. What is 721 - 207 _____
   A. 515
   B. 514
   C. 513
   D. 516

40. What is 474 + 811 _____
   A. 1286
   B. 1285
   C. 1287
   D. 1284

41. What is 300 - 415 _____
    A. -114
    B. -115
    C. -113
    D. -116

42. What is 258 + 561 _____
    A. 820
    B. 819
    C. 818
    D. 821

43. What is 674 + 121 _____
    A. 795
    B. 796
    C. 794
    D. 797

44. What is 824 - 705 _____
    A. 121
    B. 120
    C. 118
    D. 119

45. What is 966 - 314 _____
    A. 654
    B. 653
    C. 651
    D. 652

46. What is 381 + 254 _____
    A. 634
    B. 637
    C. 636
    D. 635

47. What is 140 - 209 _____
    A. -67
    B. -70
    C. -69
    D. -68

48. What is 548 + 279 _____
    A. 826
    B. 828
    C. 829
    D. 827

Place Value Quiz

1. What digit is in the hundreds place in the number 8234?
   - A. 2
   - B. 4
   - C. 5
   - D. 3

2. What digit is in the units place in the number 7382?
   - A. 4
   - B. 3
   - C. 5
   - D. 2

3. What digit is in the thousands place in the number 7820?
   - A. 9
   - B. 7
   - C. 8
   - D. 0

4. What digit is in the thousands place in the number 6729?
   - A. 7
   - B. 8
   - C. 9
   - D. 6

5. What digit is in the hundreds place in the number 5115?
   - A. 2
   - B. 3
   - C. 4
   - D. 1

6. What digit is in the units place in the number 8533?
   - A. 4
   - B. 6
   - C. 5
   - D. 3

7. What digit is in the tens place in the number 2581?
   - A. 9
   - B. 8
   - C. 0
   - D. 1

8. What digit is in the units place in the number 7307?
   - A. 7
   - B. 0
   - C. 8
   - D. 9

9. What digit is in the hundreds place in the number 5799?

   A. 9

   B. 7

   C. 8

   D. 0

10. What digit is in the thousands place in the number 7556?

   A. 8

   B. 0

   C. 9

   D. 7

11. What digit is in the hundreds place in the number 8710?

   A. 8

   B. 9

   C. 7

   D. 0

12. What digit is in the tens place in the number 9748?

   A. 4

   B. 7

   C. 5

   D. 6

13. What digit is in the tens place in the number 5676?

   A. 9

   B. 7

   C. 8

   D. 0

14. What digit is in the thousands place in the number 5059?

   A. 8

   B. 6

   C. 5

   D. 7

15. What digit is in the hundreds place in the number 2193?

   A. 1

   B. 2

   C. 4

   D. 3

16. What digit is in the thousands place in the number 9383?

   A. 1

   B. 2

   C. 0

   D. 9

ANSWERS

Page 1:   Counting Patterns: Count by 5s

1.

359	364	369	374	379

2.

844	849	854	859	864

3.

743	748	753	758	763

4.

333	338	343	348	353

5.

91	96	101	106	111

6.

634	639	644	649	654

7.

317	322	327	332	337

8.

616	621	626	631	636

9.

136	141	146	151	156

10.

483	488	493	498	503

11.

459	464	469	474	479

12.

612	617	622	627	632

13.

101	106	111	116	121

14.

202	207	212	217	222

15.

951	956	961	966	971

16.

361	366	371	376	381

17.

395	400	405	410	415

18.

345	350	355	360	365

19.

367	372	377	382	387

20.

837	842	847	852	857

21.

| 801 | 806 | 811 | 816 | 821 |

22.

| 174 | 179 | 184 | 189 | 194 |

23.

| 815 | 820 | 825 | 830 | 835 |

24.

| 33 | 38 | 43 | 48 | 53 |

25.

| 141 | 146 | 151 | 156 | 161 |

26.

| 9 | 14 | 19 | 24 | 29 |

27.

| 144 | 149 | 154 | 159 | 164 |

28.

| 214 | 219 | 224 | 229 | 234 |

29.

| 116 | 121 | 126 | 131 | 136 |

30.

| 454 | 459 | 464 | 469 | 474 |

31.

| 752 | 757 | 762 | 767 | 772 |

32.

| 461 | 466 | 471 | 476 | 481 |

33.

| 404 | 409 | 414 | 419 | 424 |

34.

| 690 | 695 | 700 | 705 | 710 |

35.

| 878 | 883 | 888 | 893 | 898 |

36.

| 698 | 703 | 708 | 713 | 718 |

37.

| 537 | 542 | 547 | 552 | 557 |

38.

| 279 | 284 | 289 | 294 | 299 |

Page 5: Counting Patterns: Count by 10s

1.

| 765 | 775 | 785 | 795 | 805 |

2.

| 716 | 726 | 736 | 746 | 756 |

3.

| 639 | 649 | 659 | 669 | 679 |

4.

| 527 | 537 | 547 | 557 | 567 |

5. | 213 | **223** | 233 | 243 | 253 |

6. | 215 | 225 | **235** | 245 | 255 |

7. | 750 | 760 | 770 | **780** | 790 |

8. | 494 | 504 | 514 | 524 | **534** |

9. | 835 | 845 | 855 | **865** | 875 |

10. | 911 | 921 | 931 | 941 | **951** |

11. | 372 | 382 | 392 | 402 | **412** |

12. | 175 | 185 | 195 | **205** | 215 |

13. | 609 | 619 | **629** | 639 | 649 |

14. | 468 | 478 | **488** | 498 | 508 |

15. | 464 | 474 | **484** | 494 | 504 |

16. | 514 | **524** | 534 | 544 | 554 |

17. | 278 | **288** | 298 | 308 | 318 |

18. | 636 | 646 | **656** | 666 | 676 |

19. | **578** | 588 | 598 | 608 | 618 |

20. | 424 | **434** | 444 | 454 | 464 |

21. | **130** | 140 | 150 | 160 | 170 |

22. | 647 | 657 | 667 | 677 | **687** |

23. | 61 | 71 | 81 | 91 | **101** |

24. | **586** | 596 | 606 | 616 | 626 |

25. | 503 | 513 | 523 | 533 | **543** |

26. | 984 | 994 | 1,004 | **1,014** | 1,024 |

27.

| 880 | 890 | 900 | 910 | 920 |

28.

| 246 | 256 | 266 | 276 | 286 |

29.

| 848 | 858 | 868 | 878 | 888 |

30.

| 173 | 183 | 193 | 203 | 213 |

31.

| 370 | 380 | 390 | 400 | 410 |

32.

| 316 | 326 | 336 | 346 | 356 |

33.

| 777 | 787 | 797 | 807 | 817 |

34.

| 551 | 561 | 571 | 581 | 591 |

35.

| 289 | 299 | 309 | 319 | 329 |

36.

| 476 | 486 | 496 | 506 | 516 |

37.

| 341 | 351 | 361 | 371 | 381 |

38.

| 16 | 26 | 36 | 46 | 56 |

Page 9:   Comparing the Numbers

1. < 2. < 3. > 4. < 5. > 6. > 7. < 8. < 9. < 10. <

11. > 12. < 13. > 14. < 15. < 16. > 17. < 18. > 19. < 20. <

21. < 22. > 23. > 24. > 25. > 26. > 27. < 28. > 29. < 30. >

31. > 32. > 33. < 34. > 35. < 36. > 37. > 38. < 39. > 40. <

41. > 42. > 43. < 44. > 45. < 46. < 47. < 48. > 49. < 50. <

Page 12:   Circle the Numbers

1. 6,291 8,564 (5,421) (9,711)

2. 4,210 (2,604) 8,051 (8,549)

3. (8,733) (2,289) 6,289 3,449

4. 7,112 (8,262) (2,323) 4,765

5. (9,936) 6,400 (5,557) 8,974

6. (2,783) 5,280 3,668 (8,174)

7. (6,607) 5,386 (4,212) 6,599

8. (9,257) 5,200 (1,244) 8,362

9. (9,457) 4,461 (3,218) 6,051

10. (1,337) (6,260) 2,105 6,005

11. 8,084 7,749 (9,011) (5,306)

12. 4,372 (8,050) 7,398 (2,046)

13. 4,281 (1,112) (9,420) 2,958

14. (5,326) (1,616) 2,581 2,010

15. 5,895 7,246 (4,104) (8,823)

16. 8,391 (2,451) (9,291) 4,532

17. (2,045) (7,926) 3,992 3,651

18. 6,043 (6,272) (4,427) 4,675

19. 5,294 (9,552) (1,889) 5,034

20. 6,269 8,362 (4,802) (8,556)

21. 7,988 (3,166) 3,318 (9,145)

22. 5,780 8,286 (4,036) (8,840)

23. 2,879 2,207 (1,155) (4,090)

24. (3,156) 3,282 (7,613) 6,633

25. (8,457) 5,478 (4,260) 6,445

26. 5,058 (4,747) 6,002 (8,008)

27. 6,684 (5,744) (7,663) 5,773

28. (9,726) 7,547 (5,741) 7,532

29. 3,444 5,547 (1,835) (6,225)

30. (9,132) (1,146) 8,752 3,758

31. 4,890 (5,151) (1,771) 4,835

32. (6,116) (1,336) 2,519 3,012

33. 2,939 5,256 (6,577) (1,791)

34. 5,101 (8,356) 4,498 (4,240)

35. (7,163) 5,309 3,460 (1,035)

36. (1,623) 8,262 (9,114) 5,332

37. 6,466 3,622 (1,646) (7,608)

38. 2,446 (2,388) 7,500 (8,310)

39. 6,725 (1,501) 2,555 (9,907)

40. 3,975 (2,166) 2,892 (6,348)

41. 4,225 (5,650) (3,834) 5,470

42. (1,969) 4,950 3,431 (5,088)

43. (2,049) 7,594 (9,061) 4,823

44. 7,686 (8,717) (3,135) 6,627

45. 6,037 6,439 (8,369) (3,493)

46. (9,690) 4,910 1,566 (1,551)

47. 7,755 (8,267) 5,065 (4,599)

48. (6,801) 4,591 (1,265) 5,996

49. (3,417) (7,112) 6,809 5,972

50. (5,428) 4,643 4,362 (2,515)

Page 15: Circle the Numbers

1. (1,191) (6,557) (6,559) (4,851)

2. (3,327) (3,677) (1,623) (8,007)

3. 8,366 (5,927) 4,870 7,536

4. (3,797) 9,398 (6,657) 9,314

5. 5,084 3,282 (7,715) 3,702

6. 9,884 (8,831) (8,287) (7,457)

7. (7,329) 4,064 2,406 1,574

8. (2,907) (7,163) 2,198 (2,393)

9. 3,076 (6,853) 3,302 4,132

10. 8,350 6,714 8,224 5,078

11. (7,643) (7,057) (6,233) (1,873)

12. (9,721) 3,728 (3,199) 4,018

13. 1,454 7,494 1,888 (3,145)

14. 6,928 1,660 (2,631) 2,360

15. 8,270 (9,101) 7,522 9,262

16. (2,271) (1,049) (6,099) 2,202

17. (4,729) 3,476 5,460 6,944

18. 7,096 (3,525) (1,963) 8,370

19. 5,058 3,636 (6,059) (3,827)

20. (3,597) (7,413) 7,736 (4,601)

21. (1,865) (8,387) (1,119) 5,413

22. 6,274 9,052 (5,465) 2,416

23. 5,222 1,942 (5,861) (9,249)

24. (9,191) (8,961) (3,807) (7,593)

25. (1,957) 5,030 7,144 7,244

26. (8,267) 6,254 (6,921) (7,929)

27. (6,531) (3,517) (8,087) (4,291)

28. 5,600 (8,803) 8,762 (1,857)

29. (2,365) (3,921) (8,397) (3,883)

30. 9,930 1,686 5,928 5,676

31. (8,011) 4,044 2,722 6,154

32. (7,663) 2,714 9,178 (6,097)

33. (9,829) (8,465) (2,869) (8,567)

34. (1,269) 1,492 (6,333) 5,610

35. (2,465) 3,190 (8,881) 3,756

36. (1,965) (2,173) (6,815) 6,418

37. (3,179) 5,004 (7,883) 6,270

38. (1,563) (9,923) (7,663) (1,271)

39. 9,102 (2,467) (9,233) (5,223)

40. 4,532 (1,767) (1,265) 4,816

41. (4,339) (2,989) 4,462 (7,135)

42. 6,934 (1,195) (1,587) (1,873)

43. (7,587) (3,787) (2,417) (7,739)

44. 2,804 (3,171) 4,710 (6,837)

45. (7,229) (6,303) 3,974 (3,659)

46. 4,830 (3,907) (5,533) (9,905)

47. 1,802 2,598 9,464 (8,801)

48. 2,258 2,110 (2,077) 1,698

49. 2,924 (5,065) (9,417) 8,976

50. (7,711) (9,679) (9,483) 2,984

1. (4,416) (7,010) (8,682) (7,776)
2. (8,506) 9,923 (8,466) 6,931

3. (7,756) (3,396) (7,994) (8,228)
4. (7,792) (7,606) 9,985 1,431

5. 7,455 4,557 6,333 (5,336)
6. (1,730) 2,785 (9,614) 6,477

7. 2,709 1,719 (5,814) 7,739
8. 3,753 (5,734) (9,126) 7,549

9. (6,820) (1,990) (9,242) 7,819
10. (5,224) (7,756) 2,399 (1,878)

11. 4,131 (3,532) (2,044) (8,862)
12. (4,116) 3,849 (3,906) (5,318)

13. (5,080) 8,985 (2,520) (4,154)
14. (4,346) 5,147 2,253 (2,630)

15. (7,396) 3,205 6,067 7,787
16. 5,109 1,727 4,177 (3,022)

17. (4,270) (1,444) (2,408) (6,802)
18. (8,364) 3,165 (6,206) 9,699

19. (3,158) 5,455 (2,204) 8,197
20. 1,741 (1,752) 3,361 8,859

21. (7,812) (1,496) (3,658) 4,767
22. (4,214) 5,971 (4,202) 2,673

23. (9,736) 7,611 1,423 3,019
24. 2,689 4,611 6,769 (3,404)

25. (9,354) (9,022) 5,591 3,671
26. 2,441 7,103 (6,954) (2,914)

27. (3,778) 2,821 (1,996) 8,891
28. (3,942) (4,056) 1,889 (6,644)

29. 9,843 7,207 (9,974) (4,612)
30. (8,068) (9,410) (8,808) (8,298)

31. 7,241 9,735 (7,066) (1,752)

32. 2,741 4,187 8,009 (8,546)

33. 8,685 (8,800) 8,843 (2,718)

34. (6,160) (9,690) (7,418) (1,708)

35. (4,542) (1,744) (1,988) (2,392)

36. 4,975 5,311 (8,730) (6,680)

37. 6,721 4,779 3,175 5,481

38. 4,637 (3,156) 5,335 (9,944)

39. 1,213 7,293 (6,430) 2,705

40. 1,037 6,201 (1,172) 9,591

41. 4,811 3,449 1,205 5,141

42. 5,213 (9,170) 1,483 1,153

43. 9,789 9,265 (1,070) (7,324)

44. 8,421 7,415 (4,322) (2,930)

45. (2,004) 1,385 (5,030) (7,962)

46. 2,011 (3,528) (4,908) 6,529

47. (4,464) (8,898) 2,505 (8,866)

48. 4,259 (5,712) (1,670) (8,340)

49. 1,571 2,397 7,581 2,525

50. 5,105 4,589 2,467 7,551

Page 30: Missing Numbers: Between

1. 4293 **2.** 5688 **3.** 3085 **4.** 2523 **5.** 3969 **6.** 1701 **7.** 2170

8. 8573 **9.** 8534 **10.** 1676 **11.** 7659 **12.** 6888 **13.** 8588 **14.** 6748

15. 9826 **16.** 7818 **17.** 8911 **18.** 4663 **19.** 7830 **20.** 4440 **21.** 7369

22. 5891 **23.** 5008 **24.** 7164 **25.** 3815 **26.** 3982 **27.** 3910 **28.** 9877

29. 6124 **30.** 6772 **31.** 2257 **32.** 3961 **33.** 6670 **34.** 1733 **35.** 8537

36. 4444 **37.** 1233 **38.** 8933 **39.** 6716 **40.** 1065 **41.** 5555 **42.** 4203

43. 8804 **44.** 4499 **45.** 7588 **46.** 3859 **47.** 3757 **48.** 5192 **49.** 5739

50. 4082   **51.** 1285   **52.** 9808   **53.** 2850   **54.** 1197   **55.** 7207   **56.** 5954

57. 1552   **58.** 5793   **59.** 2293   **60.** 3361   **61.** 9776   **62.** 7092   **63.** 6724

64. 6241   **65.** 1028   **66.** 4213   **67.** 4047   **68.** 7285   **69.** 8569   **70.** 2684

71. 7193   **72.** 6549   **73.** 7023   **74.** 6663   **75.** 8282   **76.** 1581   **77.** 2357

78. 1941   **79.** 6376

Page 21:   Missing Numbers: Before and After

1. 7498 7500   **2.** 8734 8736   **3.** 8662 8664   **4.** 7710 7712

5. 5945 5947   **6.** 2909 2911   **7.** 5288 5290   **8.** 7742 7744

9. 3082 3084   **10.** 2413 2415   **11.** 9528 9530   **12.** 1559 1561

13. 8857 8859   **14.** 6484 6486   **15.** 1641 1643   **16.** 8397 8399

17. 6700 6702   **18.** 3479 3481   **19.** 6097 6099   **20.** 7149 7151

21. 8956 8958   **22.** 8921 8923   **23.** 2648 2650   **24.** 7041 7043

25. 8572 8574   **26.** 2721 2723   **27.** 1905 1907   **28.** 4730 4732

29. 5064 5066   **30.** 5192 5194   **31.** 4662 4664   **32.** 3316 3318

33. 3815 3817   **34.** 7016 7018   **35.** 8835 8837   **36.** 3433 3435

37. 7821 7823   **38.** 2474 2476   **39.** 3941 3943   **40.** 1038 1040

41. 2655 2657   **42.** 9328 9330   **43.** 7523 7525   **44.** 4067 4069

45. 1587 1589   **46.** 2997 2999   **47.** 8955 8957   **48.** 2744 2746

49. 1753 1755   **50.** 2639 2641   **51.** 8555 8557   **52.** 1429 1431

53. 1393 1395   **54.** 9148 9150   **55.** 4475 4477   **56.** 2695 2697

57. 7009 7011   **58.** 8310 8312   **59.** 1481 1483   **60.** 9176 9178

61. 4869 4871   **62.** 9384 9386   **63.** 8682 8684   **64.** 9978 9980

65. 4261 4263   **66.** 5705 5707   **67.** 4464 4466   **68.** 5729 5731

69. 6789 6791   **70.** 7420 7422   **71.** 3278 3280   **72.** 7274 7276

73. 6148 6150   **74.** 3040 3042   **75.** 8872 8874   **76.** 8665 8667

77. 4045 4047   **78.** 9842 9844   **79.** 7685 7687

Page 31: Double Digit Addition

1. 160   **2.** 122   **3.** 47   **4.** 55   **5.** 71   **6.** 98   **7.** 106   **8.** 134

9. 156   **10.** 159   **11.** 114   **12.** 52   **13.** 116   **14.** 140   **15.** 118   **16.** 98

17. 151   **18.** 46   **19.** 66   **20.** 126   **21.** 148   **22.** 108   **23.** 89   **24.** 141

25. 166   **26.** 62   **27.** 59   **28.** 91   **29.** 75   **30.** 103   **31.** 115   **32.** 66

33. 89   **34.** 101   **35.** 144   **36.** 98   **37.** 50   **38.** 89   **39.** 169   **40.** 77

41. 103   **42.** 113   **43.** 63   **44.** 163   **45.** 123   **46.** 67   **47.** 117   **48.** 152

49. 91   **50.** 161   **51.** 26   **52.** 53   **53.** 117   **54.** 53   **55.** 82   **56.** 130

57. 29   **58.** 117   **59.** 80   **60.** 119   **61.** 131   **62.** 96   **63.** 73   **64.** 144

65. 69   **66.** 194   **67.** 57   **68.** 111   **69.** 40   **70.** 111   **71.** 179   **72.** 137

73. 33   **74.** 169   **75.** 115   **76.** 114   **77.** 133   **78.** 83   **79.** 153   **80.** 101

81. 160   **82.** 98   **83.** 116   **84.** 126   **85.** 92   **86.** 42   **87.** 52   **88.** 93

89. 72   **90.** 97   **91.** 145   **92.** 117   **93.** 109   **94.** 112   **95.** 108   **96.** 116

97. 75   **98.** 104   **99.** 49   **100.** 111

Page 35: Three-Digit Addition

1. 1,753   **2.** 615   **3.** 875   **4.** 1,148   **5.** 1,246   **6.** 1,628

7. 1,538   **8.** 746   **9.** 1,199   **10.** 1,669   **11.** 1,015   **12.** 581

13. 1,483   **14.** 1,573   **15.** 1,691   **16.** 857   **17.** 838   **18.** 1,055

19. 808	**20.** 914	**21.** 1,544	**22.** 1,343	**23.** 1,337	**24.** 1,440
25. 1,465	**26.** 1,519	**27.** 1,135	**28.** 1,362	**29.** 959	**30.** 1,223
31. 1,440	**32.** 1,098	**33.** 1,028	**34.** 1,137	**35.** 454	**36.** 881
37. 676	**38.** 1,133	**39.** 1,537	**40.** 815	**41.** 1,103	**42.** 1,038
43. 895	**44.** 984	**45.** 1,439	**46.** 463	**47.** 1,452	**48.** 1,746
49. 1,438	**50.** 1,473	**51.** 459	**52.** 1,191	**53.** 877	**54.** 618
55. 613	**56.** 1,530	**57.** 1,844	**58.** 527	**59.** 903	**60.** 336
61. 923	**62.** 596	**63.** 358	**64.** 1,267	**65.** 934	**66.** 1,237
67. 1,700	**68.** 924	**69.** 1,135	**70.** 1,454	**71.** 1,344	**72.** 876
73. 653	**74.** 501	**75.** 1,156	**76.** 1,097	**77.** 1,276	**78.** 904
79. 1,206	**80.** 885	**81.** 829	**82.** 1,716	**83.** 747	**84.** 1,181
85. 1,312	**86.** 1,277	**87.** 1,508	**88.** 1,020	**89.** 1,170	**90.** 1,813
91. 1,332	**92.** 1,134	**93.** 1,333	**94.** 1,048	**95.** 1,380	**96.** 1,391
97. 1,309	**98.** 1,266	**99.** 814	**100.** 1,107		

Page 39: Double Digit Subtraction

1. 18	**2.** 10	**3.** 6	**4.** 9	**5.** 17	**6.** 19	**7.** 2	**8.** 9	**9.** 19
10. 8	**11.** 26	**12.** 8	**13.** 1	**14.** 31	**15.** 6	**16.** 21	**17.** 65	**18.** 20
19. 1	**20.** 3	**21.** 13	**22.** 33	**23.** 25	**24.** 18	**25.** 5	**26.** 35	**27.** 10
28. 45	**29.** 25	**30.** 8	**31.** 32	**32.** 45	**33.** 5	**34.** 28	**35.** 8	**36.** 23
37. 43	**38.** 1	**39.** 32	**40.** 12	**41.** 22	**42.** 49	**43.** 7	**44.** 33	**45.** 22
46. 45	**47.** 1	**48.** 34	**49.** 33	**50.** 29	**51.** 4	**52.** 7	**53.** 3	**54.** 6
55. 31	**56.** 32	**57.** 18	**58.** 24	**59.** 43	**60.** 81	**61.** 10	**62.** 54	**63.** 23

64. 3 **65.** 1 **66.** 49 **67.** 21 **68.** 4 **69.** 27 **70.** 10 **71.** 32 **72.** 2

73. 13 **74.** 33 **75.** 67 **76.** 9 **77.** 30 **78.** 9 **79.** 8 **80.** 30 **81.** 6

82. 5 **83.** 33 **84.** 11 **85.** 1 **86.** 53 **87.** 6 **88.** 11 **89.** 27 **90.** 4

91. 82 **92.** 4 **93.** 9 **94.** 13 **95.** 19

Page 43: Three-Digit Subtraction

1. 44 **2.** 12 **3.** 46 **4.** 446 **5.** 277 **6.** 44 **7.** 103 **8.** 374

9. 46 **10.** 26 **11.** 95 **12.** 393 **13.** 339 **14.** 590 **15.** 567 **16.** 255

17. 145 **18.** 111 **19.** 0 **20.** 298 **21.** 205 **22.** 269 **23.** 23 **24.** 206

25. 211 **26.** 119 **27.** 61 **28.** 123 **29.** 40 **30.** 250 **31.** 51 **32.** 440

33. 83 **34.** 94 **35.** 65 **36.** 2 **37.** 335 **38.** 56 **39.** 127 **40.** 147

41. 3 **42.** 281 **43.** 37 **44.** 125 **45.** 396 **46.** 427 **47.** 260 **48.** 15

49. 704 **50.** 377 **51.** 61 **52.** 31 **53.** 102 **54.** 289 **55.** 157 **56.** 88

57. 64 **58.** 15 **59.** 878 **60.** 4 **61.** 43 **62.** 334 **63.** 195 **64.** 205

65. 16 **66.** 631 **67.** 89 **68.** 131 **69.** 228 **70.** 48

Page 46: Mixed Two-Digit Practice

1. 958 **2.** 56 **3.** 54 **4.** 101 **5.** 1,007 **6.** 1,029 **7.** 1,325

8. 609 **9.** 238 **10.** 3 **11.** 514 **12.** 139 **13.** 187 **14.** 1,276

15. 1,212 **16.** 77 **17.** 52 **18.** 530 **19.** 175 **20.** 29 **21.** 871

22. 322 **23.** 616 **24.** 189 **25.** 1,054 **26.** 284 **27.** 451 **28.** 53

29. 75 **30.** 801 **31.** 652 **32.** 1,155 **33.** 399 **34.** 23 **35.** 285

36. 54 **37.** 1,555 **38.** 12 **39.** 0 **40.** 410 **41.** 1,391 **42.** 112

43. 42 **44.** 135 **45.** 199 **46.** 1,191 **47.** 942 **48.** 830 **49.** 63

50. 100   **51.** 737   **52.** 720   **53.** 1,284   **54.** 278   **55.** 1,259   **56.** 1,016

57. 799   **58.** 1,686   **59.** 180   **60.** 809   **61.** 1,245   **62.** 1,324   **63.** 486

64. 23   **65.** 1,178   **66.** 703   **67.** 234   **68.** 1,157   **69.** 1,530   **70.** 1,810

71. 239   **72.** 1,694   **73.** 1,450   **74.** 1,228   **75.** 310   **76.** 1,110

Page 50: Addition with Regrouping

1. 1,510   **2.** 1,476   **3.** 1,510   **4.** 1,312   **5.** 1,121   **6.** 1,613   **7.** 1,460

8. 1,322   **9.** 1,113   **10.** 1,281   **11.** 1,181   **12.** 1,230   **13.** 1,315   **14.** 1,116

15. 1,120   **16.** 1,120   **17.** 1,620   **18.** 1,126   **19.** 1,111   **20.** 1,228   **21.** 1,112

22. 1,510   **23.** 1,641   **24.** 1,215   **25.** 1,630   **26.** 1,111   **27.** 1,413   **28.** 1,110

29. 1,385   **30.** 1,220   **31.** 1,150   **32.** 1,666   **33.** 1,132   **34.** 1,153   **35.** 1,112

36. 1,210   **37.** 1,314   **38.** 1,116   **39.** 1,332   **40.** 1,322   **41.** 1,710   **42.** 1,616

43. 1,260   **44.** 1,311   **45.** 1,125   **46.** 1,720   **47.** 1,170   **48.** 1,622   **49.** 1,110

50. 1,435   **51.** 1,124   **52.** 1,130   **53.** 1,510   **54.** 1,431   **55.** 1,241   **56.** 1,542

Page 53: Subtraction with Regrouping

1. 88   **2.** 454   **3.** 88   **4.** 219   **5.** 237   **6.** 86   **7.** 228   **8.** 257

9. 278   **10.** 66   **11.** 68   **12.** 158   **13.** 67   **14.** 329   **15.** 279   **16.** 89

17. 615   **18.** 77   **19.** 519   **20.** 165   **21.** 369   **22.** 275   **23.** 325   **24.** 55

25. 49   **26.** 107   **27.** 238   **28.** 4   **29.** 207   **30.** 88   **31.** 66   **32.** 59

33. 39   **34.** 207   **35.** 66   **36.** 159   **37.** 269   **38.** 445   **39.** 238   **40.** 68

41. 122   **42.** 159   **43.** 267   **44.** 435   **45.** 539   **46.** 369   **47.** 69   **48.** 189

49. 215   **50.** 78   **51.** 219   **52.** 387   **53.** 89   **54.** 7   **55.** 325   **56.** 27

57. 246   **58.** 19   **59.** 259   **60.** 69   **61.** 59   **62.** 389   **63.** 49   **64.** 139

65. 58 **66.** 318 **67.** 448 **68.** 128 **69.** 214 **70.** 33 **71.** 343 **72.** 37

73. 37 **74.** 228 **75.** 9 **76.** 87

Page 57: Double Digit Three-Addends

1. 167 **2.** 192 **3.** 190 **4.** 143 **5.** 168 **6.** 117 **7.** 118 **8.** 109

9. 128 **10.** 154 **11.** 178 **12.** 153 **13.** 147 **14.** 126 **15.** 162 **16.** 160

17. 187 **18.** 174 **19.** 173 **20.** 155 **21.** 167 **22.** 183 **23.** 109 **24.** 185

25. 201 **26.** 123 **27.** 268 **28.** 177 **29.** 168 **30.** 176 **31.** 183 **32.** 159

33. 220 **34.** 204 **35.** 96 **36.** 120 **37.** 156 **38.** 129 **39.** 222 **40.** 151

41. 216 **42.** 168 **43.** 218 **44.** 135 **45.** 106 **46.** 247 **47.** 167 **48.** 101

49. 152 **50.** 200 **51.** 131 **52.** 100 **53.** 122 **54.** 162 **55.** 241 **56.** 167

57. 211 **58.** 48 **59.** 224 **60.** 225 **61.** 258 **62.** 185 **63.** 216 **64.** 183

65. 84 **66.** 221 **67.** 79 **68.** 134 **69.** 88 **70.** 112 **71.** 148 **72.** 172

73. 214 **74.** 167 **75.** 136 **76.** 142 **77.** 209 **78.** 207 **79.** 122 **80.** 167

81. 133 **82.** 140 **83.** 185 **84.** 201 **85.** 193 **86.** 48 **87.** 235 **88.** 138

89. 184 **90.** 83 **91.** 65 **92.** 127

Page 63: Can you Make 1000?

1. 986 **2.** 976 **3.** 992 **4.** 996 **5.** 993 **6.** 962 **7.** 998 **8.** 984

9. 982 **10.** 981 **11.** 973 **12.** 988 **13.** 966 **14.** 994 **15.** 970 **16.** 991

17. 963 **18.** 997 **19.** 989 **20.** 995 **21.** 971 **22.** 972 **23.** 983 **24.** 961

25. 985 **26.** 965 **27.** 968 **28.** 978 **29.** 980 **30.** 990 **31.** 964 **32.** 987

33. 960 **34.** 967 **35.** 979 **36.** 969

Page 65: Place Value

1. 6 thousands	**2.** 0 tens	**3.** 4 ones	**4.** 0 tens
5. 3 ones	**6.** 4 thousands	**7.** 0 ones	**8.** 2 hundreds
9. 6 thousands	**10.** 1 hundred	**11.** 6 ones	**12.** 3 hundreds
13. 8 thousands	**14.** 5 ones	**15.** 1 ten	**16.** 8 thousands
17. 8 hundreds	**18.** 6 thousands	**19.** 2 hundreds	**20.** 5 ones
21. 1 thousand	**22.** 7 ones	**23.** 3 ones	**24.** 1 thousand
25. 7 thousands	**26.** 2 thousands	**27.** 8 thousands	**28.** 1 thousand
29. 0 tens	**30.** 2 tens	**31.** 8 tens	**32.** 5 thousands
33. 5 ones	**34.** 3 hundreds	**35.** 9 thousands	**36.** 6 thousands
37. 2 thousands	**38.** 5 thousands	**39.** 5 ones	**40.** 4 tens
41. 9 hundreds	**42.** 6 tens	**43.** 6 thousands	**44.** 0 tens
45. 2 hundreds	**46.** 5 hundreds	**47.** 6 ones	**48.** 9 ones
49. 5 tens	**50.** 9 tens	**51.** 2 tens	**52.** 8 ones

Page 68: Place Value: Expanded Notation

1. 1,583	**2.** 8,548	**3.** 6,002	**4.** 2,191	**5.** 9,775	**6.** 7,924
7. 1,378	**8.** 8,720	**9.** 2,721	**10.** 8,219	**11.** 1,558	**12.** 9,252
13. 4,606	**14.** 7,439	**15.** 4,329	**16.** 1,354	**17.** 2,333	**18.** 8,244
19. 9,905	**20.** 7,627	**21.** 1,346	**22.** 4,315	**23.** 7,075	**24.** 4,342
25. 1,931	**26.** 4,722	**27.** 2,645	**28.** 7,097	**29.** 4,813	**30.** 8,604
31. 9,396	**32.** 5,527	**33.** 2,833	**34.** 5,010	**35.** 4,039	**36.** 3,454
37. 6,357	**38.** 2,964	**39.** 2,195	**40.** 4,735	**41.** 2,774	**42.** 1,511

43. 5,539	**44.** 7,077	**45.** 6,287	**46.** 2,374	**47.** 3,584	**48.** 7,721
49. 2,745	**50.** 9,174	**51.** 7,647	**52.** 9,626	**53.** 6,741	**54.** 9,709
55. 8,537	**56.** 7,267	**57.** 2,474	**58.** 2,660	**59.** 1,260	**60.** 6,054
61. 6,279					

Page 75: Addition and Subtraction Quiz

1. 828	**13.** 1720	**25.** 1506	**37.** -74
2. 1242	**14.** 440	**26.** -526	**38.** 1204
3. 328	**15.** 936	**27.** -312	**39.** 514
4. 1081	**16.** -186	**28.** 1572	**40.** 1285
5. -446	**17.** 1460	**29.** 1908	**41.** -115
6. 490	**18.** 721	**30.** -85	**42.** 819
7. 381	**19.** -203	**31.** 1001	**43.** 795
8. 524	**20.** 784	**32.** 1290	**44.** 119
9. 285	**21.** -613	**33.** -257	**45.** 652
10. 316	**22.** -2	**34.** -105	**46.** 635
11. 1510	**23.** 449	**35.** -135	**47.** -69
12. 939	**24.** 867	**36.** 1849	**48.** 827

Page 81: Place Value Quiz

1. 2	**5.** 1	**9.** 7	**13.** 7
2. 2	**6.** 3	**10.** 7	**14.** 5
3. 7	**7.** 8	**11.** 7	**15.** 1
4. 6	**8.** 7	**12.** 4	**16.** 9